# GREAT RIDES ACCORDING TO G

Also by Geraint Thomas with Tom Fordyce

*The World of Cycling According to G*
*The Tour According to G*
*Mountains According to G*

# GREAT RIDES
## ACCORDING
## TO G

## GERAINT THOMAS

Written with Tom Fordyce

QUERCUS

First published in Great Britain in 2023 by

QUERCUS

Quercus Editions Ltd
Carmelite House
50 Victoria Embankment
London EC4Y 0DZ

An Hachette UK company

A CIP catalogue record for this book is available
from the British Library

HB ISBN 978 1 52943 421 7
Ebook ISBN 978 1 52943 422 4

10 9 8 7 6 5 4 3

Typeset by CC Book Production
Printed and bound in Great Britain by Clays Ltd, Elcograf S.p.A.

Papers used by Quercus are from well-managed forests and other responsible sources.

This book is for everyone who loves riding their bike as much as I do. Never stop adventuring.

# Contents

# Contents

# Prologue

You never feel worse after a bike ride. Someone pointed this out to me the other day and it's true, isn't it? It may have been sunny. You may have got soaked. You could be on an old familiar loop or new roads far from home. You might have smashed out some efforts in pursuit of a new goal or better time, or just cruised along, chatting to a couple of friends, stopping halfway round for coffee.

It doesn't really matter. When you get home again, something has changed in your day. You've sucked in fresh air. You've escaped the same old four walls. You've felt the wind on your face and maybe the rain or sleet too, but you've felt something – blood pumping, legs moving, the road slipping past underneath your wheels. You've achieved something, no matter what else might be going on. You might be hungry and tired and damp. You might not have gone as far as you had hoped or got there as fast as you would have liked, but you've still done it. You've still escaped. You feel different to how you did before.

That's what this book is about, really: all those adventures you can have on your bike. The routes you used to do. The ones you've loved. The ones that challenged you or thrilled you or maybe even scared you a little bit. The benign ones and the monsters. The ones you've heard about and would love to take on; the ones in places you've never been to, but dream about now that you know.

It's about practicalities too, of course, because we're practical people when we ride. Knowing which turning to take, where the wind might be coming from and what the road surface will be like. The layers of clothing you should wear, the number of bottles you'll need and where you can refill them. Where you can stop for a coffee that's worth it for the taste as well as the caffeine.

It's about the culture, because we ride through the real world: the towns and villages, the history and the vibes. It's about memories of previous rides and hopes for those ahead. It's about conversations with those riding alongside you and the shared experiences that come your way: the big views, the near misses, the laughs, the daft mistakes. It's about how you felt that day and how your bike felt underneath you and all the things you could do together.

I've chosen a big old mix here, with rides from different

times in my life and different parts of the world. There are some proper long ones and some easier ones; some that take you high and some that stay low; some that start at one and end at the other. I've picked the brains of esteemed team-mates and friends to add some extra sauce on top, too.

It's a good list, I think. I've tried to give you enough information that if you want to take them on, you'll find almost everything you need here. Just add your legs and a generous serving of effort. If you want to do it vicariously instead, there's plenty of tales and adventure too, and if you want me to ride a few miles on your behalf, I'm more than happy to do so.

Dive in. Zip up your jersey, fill your bottles and head out. Get ready to feel good. Get ready to feel better.

# Learning
# the Ropes

# In the Vale

A good ride will always be about memories. Sometimes it's about creating them – a route you'll never forget, a day full of stories and good times with great friends. If you're lucky, as a pro, it might be a training day you'll look back on and think, yep, that was one of the days that won me that big race three months down the road. If you're luckier still it might be the big race itself. I'll always remember the road to La Rosière, where I won to go into yellow on the 2018 Tour, and 31km of damp road to a little town in the far south-west called Espelette, where I held on in the final time-trial and knew, finally, that the Tour was mine.

And then there are the days when you retrace old adventures; days when you know where you're going from old instinct, where each rise in the road and little village and view takes you back to a time when it was all so different; when you were starting out and had no real idea where all this was taking you, and you were just fine with that, as long as your mum was doing a roast dinner for when you got back home.

That's what it's like when I ride out of my home town of Cardiff into the lanes of the Vale of Glamorgan. Cardiff is the best kind of capital city – big and small at the same time, contrasting areas but the same vibe, enough to keep you there but never more than fifteen minutes on your bike from open countryside. From Llandaff on the western side of the city, where my house is now, you're into the lanes in no time at all. All those times as a kid when I would shut the door behind me at the family home in Birchgrove, cut across the suburban streets to here, and feel the freedom as the roads opened up, the cars thinned out and we picked up pace.

To be fair, there are other memories, too, like the time when I signed up for a charity ride called Castles and Cathedrals for a local homeless charity, the route starting at Sa's old school, Ysgol Gyfun Gymraeg Plasmawr. We were supposed to be there for 8 a.m., which would have been fine had it not been October and the middle of my very short off-season. On-season means eating carefully and drinking nothing. There is no hint of careful or nothing in off-season. Hence waking up at 7.50 a.m., hungover, phone going berserk.

I got there for 8.02 a.m., which I thought was a decent

rescue effort. I hadn't washed and my kit may not have been clean, and I was holding two slices of bread and jam in one hand, but the lanes were still welcoming and the ride a success. It's not always how you start, but how you finish.

So we take Pwllmelin Road out of Llandaff, which turns into Pentrebane Road, heading due west. We go over the crossroads, with St Fagan's cricket club on your left, riding on to St Brides-super-Ely and Peterston-super-Ely, turning right at Gwern-y-Steeple to cut across to Welsh St Donats and enter the little town of Cowbridge from the north, on the Maendy Road.

It's never too busy leaving town on these roads. You'll pass cars going the other way if it's the morning, but not heading away from the city. The roads are up and down, and seldom flat for long. In summertime the hedges and trees alongside you will have grown high, keeping you protected from any weather. In spring and autumn the only thing to watch out for is when the farmers have been cutting the hedges with their big trimmers and there are hawthorn spikes all over the road, ready to bury themselves in your tyres. Take spare inner tubes, take a rain jacket. It never gets too cold round here and you'll always be on the pedals, up the little climbs or battling the heavy roads, but the rain is seldom far away. Rug up as you choose and remember: there is no such thing as bad weather, only bad clothing choices. Should it get wet, take solace in the fact that the roads are designed to soak it up. We're not in Italy, where the first hint of a shower turns the roads into an ice-rink. Wales expects rain. Wales shrugs it off.

Another random memory, as our legs start to warm up and fire: during the first Covid lockdown in spring 2020, Sa, Macs and I just made it back to Cardiff as France shut down. The first week we were home, I headed out along this route to do a few sprints. I launched into one from a slow start with a gear ratio of 53-13, lost my chain and veered left, straight into a bush.

It could have been worse. I managed to hold it upright. I managed not to hit my knackers on the stem of my handlebars. I managed not to swerve into the path of the car coming past. But I did clout my knee, and a phone call with my coach at the time, Tim Kerrison, led to a sensible decision: let's take it easy for a while. There are no races in the immediate future. Take time off every now and then. Be around to spend extra time with your family.

Ever since, that particular lane reminds me of Covid, but it's seldom negative for long round here. The villages you pass through are lovely and the pubs are nice places to meet friends who might be driving out instead. There's the Hare and Hounds in Aberthin, on the edge of Cowbridge, or there's the White Lion, just north of Maendy. Both serve great food.

They're also a good place for the less ride-ready to rest up and get their legs back. The days after my Tour win in 2018 were fun ones. Cycling never leaves you alone to celebrate for long – there's always another race, always another training session to do – but when I bagged the biggie I was determined to do it properly, for what training session or race could top what had just happened?

I think the drinks had been flowing for about ten days when I took to these roads with my father-in-law, Eif, and Wales winger, George North. I was still in great shape from all that racing, but this window seemed perfect, and roads that had been tough as a kid suddenly paled after racing up Alpe d'Huez and Col de Portet. I just hadn't anticipated the fresh challenge that was coming my way: after riding close to 3500km around France averaging over 40kph, riding slow turned out to be harder than I'd imagined. George is a strong boy. He's also 6ft 4in and more than 40kg heavier than me. It takes some going getting over these bumps when you're packing that kind of heat. Eif? I'm not sure I even waited at the top of each small climb after a while.

As we come into Cowbridge and pass the comprehensive school on the right, it reminds me of my old mate,

Ross Hunter-Reid. We joined Maindy Flyers around the same time as kids and quickly became good friends. Ross was super-talented on the bike, a year behind me at school but chasing each other wheel to wheel whenever we raced, all the way from these lanes to our GB Academy days up in the north-west.

One of our early races together was the Manchester Youth Tour. I won my age group, Ross made the podium in his. There was an annoying amount of hanging around afterwards and we were both keen to get back to our digs. Trouble was, we didn't have our bikes, it was too far to walk and my only footwear was my cycling cleats. The solution we chose? Sharing Ross' trainers. You can't say there was no logic in it – he wore the right one and me the left, and then halfway into the run home we swapped. Now we both had the same amount of dirt and blisters on each foot. Buzzing with the genius of our plan, we raided the fridge at our digs, came across a rogue can of Stella left by one of our dads and decided to have a pop. Two seconds later it was being launched out of the skylight. Ross is in the US now, in the army, and he's due to move to the other side of the world pretty soon, but here, thousands of miles away, my bike and all it can do bring him right back into my mind.

If you haven't been there before you'll like Cowbridge.

Good cafés and boutique shops for the dedicated followers of fashion. Personally I'd recommend Ground, partly because it's owned by George, but also because the coffee is great and the brunches top notch. It's an ideal place to stop as you come back round this loop a little later on. If you want to head a touch further out of town, try the Cowbridge Farm Shop on Llantwit Major Road – plenty of outside space to leave your bike, and a good spot to meet your kids if you've done your ride and want to remind yourself why you went out on your bike in the first place.

It's a gradual uphill drag as you leave Cowbridge, more houses there now than when I was a boy. Halfway up the drag out of town keep an eye out for a small road called Geraint's Way. Imagine how often I dreamt of living on that road as a kid.

At the top of the climb we hang a left and pass Llandow Circuit. Built for motor racing, it used to host bike racing on Wednesday nights in summer – road bikes, rather than the track bikes we'd use at the oval in Maindy, back in Cardiff. We loved it: such a big circuit to race around, the track wide, the bends sweeping and so quick. As a teenager you could race against actual adults, the sort of legendary local riders everyone grew up hearing about and slightly hero-worshipping. There was Owen Beckett;

there was Ian Jeremiah, who owned the Cyclopaedia bike shop on Crwys Road in Cardiff. I remember getting to the age where I could start to match a few of them and then maybe begin to put them away too. Man, that made you feel good about yourself.

It was a tight little scene in those days. When I won the Welsh Road Race Championships as a junior, I was due to ride the Five Valleys Premier Calendar a couple of weeks later – a proper big race for us in Wales, the one where we all wanted to be at our best. Perhaps sensing my desire to look good on the biggest stage, men's national champion Stuart Meek loaned me the jersey he'd had made when he won the Welsh Crit Championships. I'm not 100% it was British Cycling Federation legal, but none of us cared when it looked so good – a beautiful Welsh red with a white, red and green stripe across the chest, and a lemon yellow and pink 'Jif' inset. Was the Cardiff Jif club sponsored by a major household cleaning product? No. This was a direct dig at the rival Cardiff Ajax. Jif didn't mean sparkling bathroom tiles. It stood for 'Just in front'. That's how it was in road racing in south Wales at the time. Like downtown LA and the Cripps and Bloods, except with bikes.

Back to present day Llandow, and if you're passing during the day it's more about the karting; the angry waspy sound of those engines, the thought of how fun it would be to race them right now. But we have our own two-wheeled pleasures ahead – through Llantwit Major on the quiet B4270 and along the coast on Dimlands Road to St Donats, passing little coffee shops and ice-cream places along the beach. Then it's back north-westwards into the lanes, through the villages of Marcross and Monknash, and their big views out past the lighthouse and sand. It can be windy out here, because you're quite exposed and the rain gets carried into your face on the sea winds, but there's something nice about it, too. We ride our bikes to be out in the real world, to feel the breeze on our face, to feel more alive than we do when we're stuck indoors staring out at it instead.

It's a slightly bigger road through Wick, although it's all relative; it's only the B4265. This is where Nicole Cooke grew up. All these years later, I'll still look out for her and her mum and dad and brother as I ride through, even though her brother's a pilot out in the US and I haven't spotted Nicole there for decades.

She was the start of it all, Nicole. The great rise of British cycling, the Olympic medals, the impossible wins. I was fifteen when she won the Junior Road Race World Championships. I remember all of us riding over to Wick to see her in her rainbow jersey kit, a big welcome-home party thrown for her in the local pub. It blew my mind that someone from a place I knew could do such a thing. It made all the things that should have been out of reach for us kids from south Wales seem possible. It wasn't like a French woman winning something or even Brad Wiggins from London. It was Nicole, from just down the road. When she won Olympic road race gold in Beijing in 2008 and then the World Road Race the same year, I was well on the way on my own journey, winning gold with the team pursuit squad on the track. But it was still Nicole who started it off; her gold was the first British one of those games; she was the pioneer, the inspiration.

We ride on, towards Ogmore-by-Sea. Keep an eye out for the Fox pub, on Ewenny Road in St Brides Major. It's been bought and done up by Gavin Henson, genius of a centre for Wales, fond of refreshment afterwards. He's known to serve pints in there, so pop in if you're doing the loop.

It's typical Wales, this section from the coast back up the river estuary towards Ogmore itself: rolling roads; sheep by the roadside, all of them familiar enough with passing riders not to run in front of you in a panic as you pass; the views off to your left like a Welsh version of the cliffs of Dover. You can see villages further west up the coast in the distance. You can see kites flying on the beach, swimmers stepping through the waves and sandcastles being built.

We pass Ogmore Castle on our left, Southerndown Golf Club on our right. Peckish? Stop at Cobbles, on the north side of Ogmore. Cracking sandwiches in there, although it's rare I get to stop and fill my boots here. My food tale from this spot is another of near disaster, when I attempted to eat a Welsh cake as I rode through the railway tunnel just past Cobbles, hit a pothole and lost the one hand I had on my handlebars. Usually this means a crash. On this occasion I managed to not only re-grab the bars, but also maintain the grip I had on the Welsh cake. My whoops of delight are probably still echoing through that tunnel as you read this.

Onwards to Ewenny on the B4524. I say I don't often stop for food round here – there was one ride when I was in bits, having blown my doors off, and the Post Office corner shop here saved my bacon, as well as my pasties and pastries. I hadn't been doing efforts or even pushing that hard. I just hadn't eaten much, if anything at all, and to be fair I was slightly hungover. But as you've found out by now, these roads are heavy and you're always pushing, even if you don't want to. The menu and ingredients on offer at this Post Office are insane for a little place. Not only did I make it home that dark day, I rode back smiling and glazed of eye.

Go straight on here and you ride smack-bang into another big memory. There's a fantastic local race held here every year called the Betty Pharoah Memorial Leg-stretchers Race. It was started by Reg Pharoah, something of a cycling legend in south Wales, in honour of his late wife. You can race it as a junior or a senior, as a elite rider or fourth cat, which is the bottom of the amateur ladder.

We thought of it as the south Wales version of the Tour of Flanders. Everyone talked about it, everyone wanted to do it. I won it for the first time as a first-year junior, racing third and fourth cat seniors, riding away at the start and holding on. The next year, bumped up to the elites, I was in a group of three coming towards the finish. Me, Paul Sheppard (aka Shifty) and Stephen Roche – not the Irish superstar, but a Welsh one who rode for Rugby and specialised in cyclo-cross. There was a steep little climb as you came towards the end, quite punchy after 60km of racing, and I took them on there and then put both away in the sprint. Good times.

We're heading home now. We can follow the lanes along Wick Road from Ewenny back into Cowbridge, or turn right to come back along the coast again. If you're going straight on, you go through what I used to think of as the Vale of Glamorgan's own Death Valley. It's admittedly not quite as hot. No-one has ever fried an egg on a car bonnet here. But it's bleak and there's no-one around, and if you know what's good for you, you'll hurry straight through it.

Grab that coffee at George North's place in Cowbridge. Go back past the school and go all the way to Pontyclun on the A4222. It's a main road, but an easy one: 30mph limits, plenty of space for us as well as cars. Keep half an eye on who might be driving those cars, too. We're close to the Vale Resort hotel here, where the Welsh rugby team stay when they're training and before big matches.

There's more of a south Wales valley feel now, as we dip under the M4 and head north. Small, tough communities built around hard work and rugby. If you fancy a little more of the former, climb through the lanes to Castell Coch, scene of one of the first races I ever did, a local hill-climb in early autumn. Gradual at the bottom, steeper towards the top, it was also the scene of a cycling triumph for Sa, although I only found this out when we'd been together for some time. It was the Welsh School Championships and Sa was persuaded by a friend to team up so they could win a school award. It's all about the motivation when you're on your way to the top.

A couple more options for us before we finish. If you turn right halfway up the climb you can drop straight down back into Cardiff, or keep going all the way up to Caerphilly Mountain on Caerphilly Road or Rhiwbina Hill. The hardest way comes back in the other direction from the Caerphilly side; the Tour of Britain has come that way. This side, the Rhiwbina way, you get to ride past the Black Cock Inn, which always gave us a chuckle as kids.

At the top, views stretch everywhere. There used to be a burger van with a proper burger man vibe: greasy chips, sauces in unmarked plastic squeezy bottles, red and white striped apron. It's now a permanent structure, perhaps reflecting what excellent business the van always seemed to do. You can eat what you like here, because the descent into Cardiff is smooth and fast all the way down – and at the end of a ride like this, the sensation of speed is exactly what's required.

# Up in the Gogs

Wales might not be the biggest of nations, but it still has its rivalries. The whole country comes together against the English, of course, no matter what the contest, although particularly in rugby. But, as anywhere else, there are other angles. The south and the north. Cardiff and Swansea, joined by the M4 but divided by football. Whitchurch and Llanishen schools in Cardiff, even if Llanishen hasn't produced Wales' rugby captain, its greatest ever footballer and a Tour de France winner within the space of a few school years.

There were always rumours at school of the Llanishen boys coming over to ours for a fight. Maybe they just wanted to see how good Sam Warburton and Gareth Bale were in the flesh. Maybe they just wanted to combine for the next away match at the Liberty Stadium. Regardless, we've ridden through the northern Cardiff suburbs and will ride through Swansea later in this book, so it's time to head for the Gogs.

A little explanation: Gogledd Cymru is north Wales. As a result, both its lands and the people are known colloquially in the south as Gogs. There was even an animated TV show called *Gogs* on S4C in the 1990s, featuring some primitive Stone Age-style clay figures messing about and having fun. And while I grew up in the south and have ridden out west, the north also has a place in my heart, both for its culture and for its riding.

My first adventures there came with my good mate Rob Partridge, who grew up in the Wrexham area. We would stay at his parents' house and ride west from there, into the Clwydian Range and then on into Snowdonia (now more properly known by its Welsh name, Eryri). The hills were exposed in winter and sheltered by trees in summer. It was always up or down and the roads all seemed to be twisty, but mostly it was fun, so much so that on one ride we were laughing so much as we attempted impersonations of different people that we could barely get enough oxygen in our lungs to keep pedalling. Sometimes we lost our minds in other ways. There was one old manor house called Plas Teg, on the Wrexham Road just outside Pontblyddyn, that we were so convinced was haunted that we couldn't even look at it for fear that the ghosts inside would chase us down the road.

I took some of the same roads in a few years later, on

a charity ride from the Vale of Glamorgan to Denbigh. Sa's taid, her grandfather, had died earlier that year of complications from a stroke and Alzheimer's, and we wanted to raise money for the charities that deal with both those issues. Realising that me riding 160 miles wouldn't get anyone dipping into their pockets, I decided to ride a tandem with Sa. Others in the family also joined us for spells: Sa's dad Eif, her mum Beth, her brother Rhys and his now wife Carys; my brother Alun and my best man Ian. My own dad was the only one of the amateur crew to ride the entire thing, but that was fine, and we had my aunty driving a campervan just behind the micro-peloton, so you could drop back for a snack or a snooze as required, plus my mum in a car if you needed more or fewer items of clothing.

There was one issue. Sa kept getting the hump every time someone asked if she was actually pedalling or not. To be fair, she was pedalling for most of it, at least until she started suffering from a sore bottom and had to seek assistance from a couple who offered to lend her a padded cover for her saddle. But the roads as we entered the north from mid-Wales were a joy. Even the big ones were never that busy. The last 20 miles to her taid's home town of Denbigh were super-nice. On the actual day I struggled to take all of it in – we had left the Vale at 5.30 a.m., arrived at Denbigh Cricket Club at 7 p.m., and then piled straight into a massive barbecue and a similarly large number of complementary beers – but it was great and reminded me how good the riding can be in these parts.

So it seems fitting that we should start this ride in Denbigh. You can even leave from the cricket club on Ystrad Road for total authenticity of you like, although don't count on the free cold beers. We're heading for Ruthin and, while you can take the A525 through Rhewl and be perfectly content, we're going on the backroads via Llandyrnog and Rhôs, out of town east on the Whitchurch Road, then turning right onto the B5429.

Riding through Ruthin always reminds me of another era in these hilly parts, when Sa and I had moved in together in Altrincham on the edge of Manchester, and this area was the closest part of Wales to us. The first time we drove out here visiting I met Em, Sa's uncle, before sitting in his conservatory chatting to her taid. All very normal until a 15-stone bloke arrived on a four-year-old's BMX, wearing a misfitting helmet and swimming goggles. As first impressions go, that certainly broke the ice.

A few visits later I decided to take my bike. This was an age before mapping software on your phone. You considered yourself lucky if you had Snakes. The handlebar stem-mounted Garmin was also a distant dream and the only option was going to the AA website and printing off directions from its journey planner. So Mel, one of the local boys Eif was friends with, came over and followed me in his car for the whole ride, directing me as we went along. I've no idea where we really went, but we did some cracking little roads, some of which may even feature today.

We'll take the A525 out of Ruthin and head up the Nant Y Garth pass towards Llandegla village, taking a slight right onto the A542, with the option of a coffee at the Ponderosa café if you can't wait any longer. Now we're at Horseshoe Pass, probably the jewel of the ride.

As you approach the bottom it immediately becomes clear why the road is named as it is. While it's a decent old climb – almost 6km long, an average of 5% – it's never that brutal, and the way it takes you round the inside of the hill's contour makes it a classic to tick off. The descent towards Llangollen is equally fun. Just don't have so much fun that you career into Llangollen itself. Instead, turn right before you cross the River Dee, on to the B5103, and then follow Llidiart Annie Road, with the river meandering along on your left-hand side, the busier A5 and its traffic across the other side of its banks.

It's a beautiful section of road this, almost single track in places, all the way through to the village of Carrog. It can feel similar to being out in the distant wilds of west Wales, in that the lanes can sometimes feel like farm tracks, and then you're riding straight through what feels like a farmyard, wondering if you're actually allowed to be there at all or have inadvertently trespassed up to someone's front door. But it's all good, especially when it's not raining, and while you're often pedalling hard up the rolling climbs, there are also sections like this through the valleys and along waterways, when it all suddenly seems very easy.

We're ready to head back now. Once through Carrog, take the B5436 and then turn right on the A1504 towards Bryneglwys. Rob and his mates used to call this Bonk Road, so weary would they be as teenagers doing their first long Sunday rides, running out of fuel and seeing stars, getting dropped by the middle-aged men leading the ride and left to find their own way home. From the crossroads at Llandegla, we retrace our early efforts to Ruthin and then it's once more on to the B5429 to Denbigh.

It's not a monster, this one. You won't have done much more than 50km, depending on exactly which route and back road you've decided to take. But you'll have experienced the Gogs, and that can only ever be a good thing.

# Cheshire Lanes

You have a lot of tough days as a pro cyclist. Days when your legs are heavy and your neck gets sore, days when you sort of dread it at the start and enjoy it when it's all over, when you're home and washed and fed, and your bike's propped back up against the wall and you look at it every now and then like it's a beloved pet that also has a nasty bite.

Then there are the other days. The ones when your coach says, yeah, just go and spin your legs out, ride for a couple of hours, do a few gentle efforts, but only to let yourself recover from what has been before. Those are days when your feet are light on the pedals, when you can look up and notice the scenery rather than having your nose hovering above the stem of your handlebars, when you can stop for a coffee and let the time run past and then order another one.

That's where we're going today. This is a route we used to do when I lived in Manchester and rode with the

British Olympic programme, when we were training for the team pursuit in the velodrome but getting out and about in the real lumpy, bumpy world as much as possible. It's a familiar one for anyone who lives in Manchester or Cheshire, because this is the softer part of the north, a world of quiet lanes and green hedges and big fields, of pockets of woodland and the smell of dairy cows and quite often the waste products of dairy cows too. But we're out of the city here, so we must embrace it all.

We start at the crossroads in the village of Ashley. Most people will come from further in, but this is the regular meeting point for loads of local rides, so if you're solo there'll probably be plenty of others who you can check directions with or whose wheel you can jump on. On summer evenings an impromptu chain-gang often starts here.

Maybe you've ridden out of the city, through Timperley and Hale; maybe you've wiggled and waggled from Chorlton or Stretford or Whalley Range, maybe Wilmslow or Stockport. If it's Hale, follow the Ashley Road south over the train line and under the M56 motorway until you get to the Greyhound Pub. The crossroads is just after. We're going to turn right, past the church on your right and the cricket club on your left, and follow the road as it straightens until you see the big, tall gates of the Rostherne entrance to Tatton Park.

If you're from London, think of Tatton as the Richmond Park of Cheshire. It's got deer roaming free, it's got a grand hall in the middle, it's got a number of lakes (or meres, since we're in the north) and it's got a road running through it where cars must stick to 20mph and riders can feel as safe as can be. There's a café in the courtyard of the hall if you need it, but I'd advise you to wait for what lies ahead, and follow the road as it drops down and then up again into the market town of Knutsford.

There's a possibility you might see a Premier League footballer knocking round Knutsford, if that's your thing. It's not Alderley Edge or Prestbury, where you can't move for them, but there's a fair few Manchester United, Liverpool and Manchester City stars in the bigger houses on the edge of town. There are also loads of cafés, either on Queen Street (Top Street to the locals) or King Street (Bottom Street – it'll make sense when you see them), but I'd still hold off at this point and save them for the way back in.

At the roundabout in the middle of town, head west along the A5033 as if you're going to Northwich. At the next roundabout, turn left on to Sudlow Lane, leave the town and the new estates on its fringes behind, and roll into the first of many quiet lanes.

It's lovely down here, with the most gradual of descents

over the M6 and onwards past farmhouses and thatched cottages. You can coast along, protected from the wind, never needing to get out of the saddle, riding two abreast if you're with friends, taking as much road as you want if solo. At the junction with Plumley Moor Road, go straight over and follow a smaller lane still for just under a mile until the next T junction.

I'll be honest: you can get all sorts of weather in this part of England. It's a ride to have a rain jacket tucked into your rear pocket, to keep an eye on the forecast and quite often to remind yourself that skin is waterproof. Back in the old days I remember the snow falling so hard that our coach Rod Ellingworth texted us young hopefuls to tell us not to worry about going out. Thing is, we had already done one and a half hours by then, and were sat in a café with our venti caramel macchiatos and probably some sort of cinnamon swirl or blueberry muffin. It's a different life, when you're on the track rather than the road. It's all about the power, we'd tell ourselves with each bite.

Still, the snow fell to the point where we realised it wasn't so much passing as settling deep. It should have been thirty minutes home. On this day it took well over an hour, not because we were taking it steady in the snow, but because we were young and foolish and excited and kept attacking each other on the bike and attacking each other with snowballs.

Another snow day, another adventure. This time we were doing efforts. The snow hadn't quite settled and the roads were clear. Again, because we were young, foolish and excited, we hadn't considered ice. It's a little like the youngsters I'm racing against now. We didn't overthink it, we just went for it. The inevitable happened; on one shaded bend our team-mate Ross Hunter-Reid hit what must have been a 20m section of black ice. We had no chance. We all hit the deck, all sliding into the snowy hedges via the muddy verges. There were no serious injuries, just a very cold ride home (without another single attempted effort).

Anyway, it's calmer and easier in the lanes down here than in the hills over there. If keeping out of the Peaks denies you the dramas of the Cat and Fiddle climb (see my previous book, *Mountains According to G*) or adventuring out to Flash, the highest village in England, then there is still cycling culture everywhere you look. Come out on a summer evening and you might well see riders in skin-suits on bikes with disc wheels, because the amateur time-trialling scene round here is well established and of a high standard. Just don't try to jump on anyone's wheel – it's not the done thing, and in any case we're spinning our legs out, not trying to blow the doors off again.

So turn left at the junction we were at a few paragraphs ago, back over the M6 (in Cheshire you're never that far away from a motorway, a train line or an airplane overhead, but you're never close to them for long, either) and an immediate right on to Baker's Lane. When this ends, go straight over and along Townfield Lane until you meet the A50. Directions become straightforward for a while here – you're now on Route 573 of the National Cycle Network and the blue signs are easy to follow. The A50 won't bother you for long; it's a fast road but only a single carriageway in each direction. Wait for a gap between the tractors and the Range Rovers getting angry with the tractors, and go straight over again towards Boots Green.

Depending on what sort of bike you're riding, you've got potential for a nice little side-dish here. If you go straight on at the first right-hand bend, following a small purple sign for Lauren's Ride, you'll be on a small road that narrows to a track and eventually pinches out into a bridleway into the woods. On a gravel bike? Cyclocross? You could have a whale of a time down there. It can get churned up and muddy in winter, but on a dry day, any time from April through to mid-autumn, it's a brilliant piece of singletrack, past daffodils early on and then bluebells in May, all the way to conkers as summer fades.

Road bike? Have no regrets. We're still going to have a lot of fun. You're coming into Goostrey now. Pass a general store on your right called the Trading Post and turn left on to the main road through the village, past a couple of pubs and over the bridge by the railway station. We're still on route 573 here, and we'll stay with it as we cross the A535 at Twemlow Green and continue on towards Kermincham Green in the direction of Swettenham. It's all fields and horses and houses you might quite fancy round here, the great white bowl of the space telescope at Jodrell Bank visible to your left in the gaps between hedges and farm buildings. Swettenham itself is a dead end, but there's a good pub down there if you want to turn a social ride into a truly sociable one. It's only a diversion of a mile there and a mile back, so let temptation take you where it wants.

This point in the ride takes me down memory lane again, to a ride on these roads the day after my 19th birthday. The big day itself wasn't the issue; it was the big night that followed it that proved problematic. At the time I was living in a small rented house in Manchester with Mark Cavendish and Ed Clancy, our fellow GB track riders Tom White and Matt Brammeier in a similar house

100m down the road. My birthday coincided with the Champions League final of 2005, and Liverpool's famous miracle of Istanbul. We had no reason to expect extra time, let alone penalties, but as the drama stretched out, so did the number of pints.

By the time Jerzy Dudek saved Andriy Shevchenko's feeble penalty it had gone past five and six and deep into the blurry zone. I do remember being in a branch of Subway and buying all the cookies and muffins they had left, which was quite a lot, and really pissing off the dude behind me in the queue. And I have vague recollections of being back in the house and waking up Cav and Ed, and Ed coming downstairs, and Cav staying in his room, and Matt having a food fight with the cookies and muffins. Then it's more snapshots: chairs and sofa turned upside down; trainers hanging from the lampshade; plant pot in the microwave, which a few hours later would fall out and smash as Cav made his porridge in the morning. 'Aaagggh!' (Plus a few expletives.)

All would have been fine, had a reporter not been coming over at 8 a.m. to interview us and spend the day following us around. With him would be coach Rod. There was the vacuum cleaner breaking as I was frantically hoovering up the mess at 7:45 a.m., trying not to throw up in the process. There was trying to get my cycling kit on and not being able to find my shoes. There was calling Matt and him having no idea, and then him calling me back laughing a few minute later. 'Sorry, I forgot – check the freezer.'

It was in these Cheshire lanes a couple of hours later that we tried to do the subsequent lead-out. Turns out we dropped Cav miles before we got to the virtual finish line. A wise old coach in my youth once told me, 'Fill your boots, lads. Enjoy yourself. But don't miss a training day or effort.' Well, we didn't. Cav, on the other hand, apparently didn't sleep well enough. Bless him.

I trust you will be clearer of head and conscience. Just as the road starts to descend towards the river Bollin at Swettenham, do a left down Message Lane and follow the blue signs for route 71, pretty much due east. At a T junction with Mill Lane, turn left to pick up route 55, rolling across the A34 at Marton and onwards to Gawsworth. We're getting closer to the foothills of the Peak District here; on a cold, clear winter's day you might see a line of snow on the hills away to the east and on a good summer morning you'll see the telecoms mast at the top of Croker Hill, midway between Macclesfield and Congleton, which is an excellent marker for whenever you are on this part of the Cheshire plain.

You could push on east from Gawsworth, start to climb

towards Sutton Lane Ends and Macc Forest or unlikely named Peaks villages like Wincle and Wildboarclough, but save those for another day. Instead, turn back north-west on Dark Lane towards the B5392, Siddington and then Withington Green. If you can't see the road signs, just look for what looks like the largest satellite dish in the world, because we're going right up close to Jodrell Bank this time. It's Bomish Lane you take off the briefest section of the A535, then Red Lane and a right on to Blackden Lane.

Remember that amazing piece of singletrack from earlier on? You'll pass the other end of that now, so if you fancy another joust, dive off down there and fill your boots. If not, follow this lane down to a bridge over a small river and up the other side towards the village of Over Peover – unless, that is, you like a little history on your social rides, in which case you can pop down the long drive of Peover Hall to see an impressive-looking 16th-century manor house, where World War Two hero and US maverick General Patton based himself and his staff as they trained their troops before D-Day.

Peckish? You will be. And all that self-discipline earlier in the ride can pay off now, as we take Stocks Lane for a mile or so to the A50 and turn north to get back into Knutsford. Our Cheshire Lanes loop is complete, but our refuelling is just about to begin. Top Street, Bottom Street – there are cafés and tea houses everywhere you look in this town. Eat, drink, talk nonsense; roll back through the Knutsford gate of Tatton Park and retrace your tyre marks to the start at Ashley, once again best of friends with your bike. Once again back in love with our beautiful hobby and sport.

# The Italian Job

I know the café part of these rides I've chosen generally comes halfway through the adventure or at the very end. Well, today we begin with coffee, because I always did here – and even the thought of it makes me smile.

This was the deal. A load of us younger British riders all found ourselves based in Tuscany for our various teams. There was me with Barloworld, Mark Cavendish at T-Mobile, Ben Swift with Katusha, Ian Stannard at ISM and Steve Cummings with Discovery, and Quarrata was the heart of it all, the town where most of us lived and the place where almost all our rides would begin.

The exact spot? Bar Grazia, or Bar G as we used to call it, on Piazza Risorgimento. It was either that or the café just across the square. The agreement would be to leave at 10 a.m., having had a brief discussion about where we fancied going that day. The reality was that we'd start arriving at 10 a.m., sit down for a cappuccino, move on to a brioche or two and almost certainly take in a *crostata di marmellata*, usually the apricot one. I'll never forget the taste. It was like having angels disco-dancing across your tongue.

There was never a rush to get off. Girlfriends, if you had one, were back in the UK. We were in a cycling-obsessed part of the world and we were at the peak of our cycling obsessions. We could eat more than we ever could as we got older, because attempting to win a Grand Tour seemed a ludicrous idea at that point and because a lot of us were riding the road as a subset of aiming for Olympic gold on the track in Beijing in 2008. Steve Cummings was the slight exception: slightly older, more regimented as a result, generally more of a plan. Our outlook was simple. Ride out for a little sweat, as GB coach and former Olympic medallist Max Sciandri told us to. Have fun. Relish all the heat and long descents, and the perfect coffees that Italy could offer and our home towns in Blighty never could.

Despite all the discussions and all the procrastination pastries, we would inevitably start by heading straight to the San Baronto climb. It's up there with the most famous climbs in the region, but the first time you ride it you're not entirely sure why – not because there's anything wrong with it, but because there are so many lovely climbs around there that it's hard to select a winner. I raced over it early on, in the Giro di Toscana – four days of learning the ropes and the landscape, managing to get into the break on three of those stages – and the Worlds road race in Florence in 2013 came down it, the year Rui Costa won in a sprint finish.

Coming down San Baronto we would always go full gas. We were young, we were in love, we were ignorant of the risks. You arrive in Tuscany from the UK and for some people it's the art galleries and churches of Florence or the vineyards and villas. For us it was the climbs and the descents, the hairpins and the speed you could gather rushing round the bends and plunging on ahead. We would hit 60kph without trying. We would be overtaking and undertaking. Occasionally we would be crashing wildly, but we always came back for more.

Sometimes we would play a game where no pedalling was allowed. The majority of us were of similar weight, which meant it was all about the tuck and using the slipstream of others, and how you utilised your momentum in and out of corners. If you'd seen us you would have thought we fancied ourselves as MotoGP riders. The big-boned Ian Stannard had an obvious weight advantage, but that just added to the fun.

From Casalguidi it's not a brute – 6.4km long with an average gradient of 4.6% up to just shy of 350m – but it's a hot old climb in summer. There are trees towards the top to offer shade, though, and while it can be wet in spring and autumn it's seldom cold. As with all climbs, it's not just what it offers, but what you give to it. I've used it for efforts, capacity-style ones, and it fits the bill a treat. Whichever way you decide to ride it, attack or defence, it's a good climb to start your day. You'll be warm at the top. You'll have one of Max's little sweats. You'll be ready for more.

We go straight over the top on to the SP16 towards Lamporecchio. You could go left and head towards Vinci on the SP9, and if you're not sure why then try putting the name Leonardo in front of the town. There's a museum there featuring many of his greatest hits, which I'm slightly ashamed to say I've never visited, but also honest enough to admit I'm not that disappointed in myself. I always had something else I wanted to do slightly more, even if it was lying around recovering. It's the Tuscan equivalent of never having gone up in the cable car to the absolute top of Mount Teide, and if I ever do decide to tick one of them off, it will probably be Teide, because I've ridden past that many more times than Leonardo's best-of.

It's a steeper descent towards Lamporecchio than it is a climb up to it. The Vinci road is more gradual. Both, however, are enjoyable. Head towards Vinci and you're in the trees, and it's slightly twistier and slightly longer.

You often think you're there, only to round a corner and realise it's still a fair old pedal. But it's Lamporecchio that is our destination today, and beyond that another cool Tuscan town, Montecatini Terme.

As the name might suggest, it's all about the waters here: spring water to drink, spas to soak in. Max Sciandri had another sage piece of advice: after training, boys, get yourself over there, rehydrate on the lovely water, have a little spa and jacuzzi. I did go, although I feel I didn't make the most of it as I was too busy enjoying sight of the bald Steve Cummings being forced to wear a shower cap in the pool, just because that was the rule, even though he couldn't clog up a filter if he tried.

It's the busiest part of our ride here. Italian drivers have a reputation for craziness and, in large part, it's justified. They drive close to each other. Braking is optional, indicating is on personal whim, but there's a method to their madness. It works, driving like that, when everyone else does. They're also used to cyclists. More importantly, they like cyclists. They watch pro cyclists race on TV, they watch pro cyclists race around their own streets.

I was riding the Giro with Team Sky in 2012 when stage 11 finished in Montecatini Terme. Our plan was all about Mark Cavendish and all about delivering him in the perfect position to sprint for the stage victory: me leading him out, then Pete Kennaugh, in front of me, launching the Manx Missile to the line. Sounds simple, and it was, until it went wrong on the final corner. I almost crashed, Cav lost all his speed, Tomas Vaitkus and Roberto Ferrari jumped us and Ferrari held on, even though Cav nearly caught him.

Cav was already far from a fan of Ferrari. On the third stage in Denmark, Ferrari had swerved right across the road at the finish, bringing down Cav and Taylor Phinney too. He'd then told the media that he hadn't seen what happened behind him. You don't really need to wind up Mark Cavendish – he's quite capable of doing that by himself – so Ferrari's chat, and his moves, pushed him close to self-explosion. He'd wanted to win near Quaratta. We'd all wanted him to win near Quaratta. That near-miss probably cost him the points jersey in the Giro that year, too.

Bad times in a cool place. We had another finish there on stage four of Coppi e Bartali in 2022 and again it failed to go to plan. This time we were leading out our Ineos team-mate Ethan Hayter when Mathieu van der Poel pipped us to the line, having already been in the break all day, which is a very Van der Poel thing to do. Our team still took the top three places in the points competition and won the GC with Eddie Dunbar, but I can't help thinking that Montecatini Terme still owes me a certain something.

Actually, it definitely owes me something. I was on a training ride there years ago in heavy rain. I was coming up the inside of a line of cars, loads of room to get past, when someone suddenly turned across me to park, utilising the optional indicating method. I bunny-hopped onto the pavement. I considered braking, only to realise the surface was so wet that neither stopping nor turning sharply were options. By this point I was by a brick wall, so hitting a large metal machine sticking out of it seemed like the better idea. It was only as I lay on the floor, bike sliding 20m down the road from me, shoulder in agony, that I realised the machine in question was a condom vending machine. Maybe it had done what it advertised: getting between me and an unwanted tricky situation. It just didn't feel that way as I lay there in a puddle with a bashed-up shoulder.

To Pescia and one of Steve's favourite climbs. We'll have our second coffee break here, but in contrast to our opening effort, we're not messing about here. This is a pit-stop Italian style: don't take your helmet off, don't sit down, go straight to the bar, order your espresso, throw it down the hatch hot and potent, slam your Euro coins down, march out and remount. You should be able to do the whole thing in less than three minutes. With practice and a slick barista this can become two.

It's a lovely climb, Pescia: a good road, averaging between 5 and 7%, out of the wind for most of it and a gradual ascent to a flat plateau. It's not a typically Tuscan road, either, because it's big enough for cars to pass you easily, with respect, although it becomes quieter when you reach the peak, and then it's a lovely run across the top of the mountain. Two climbs, both of them pleasant. I knew you'd enjoy this ride.

Now to drop down to Macchia. It's a twisty descent, this one, and much more stereotypically Italian: tight corners, each of them slightly different in pitch and turn, narrow in most parts, cars coming the other way that might position themselves in parts of the road you don't expect. In short, it's a road you don't want to ride too crazy. We had a day here some time in 2008 when my old Team GB track team-mate Stephen Burke found a corner tightening up on him more than he had anticipated. He was unable to adjust and ended up riding straight into a ditch. It was amusing at the time and it was still tickling me on that stage in Coppi e Bartali in 2022. As we came round it that day I instinctively recognised it as Burkey's Corner. Even as I focused on keeping my line, I could once again see him disappearing into the ditch with a slight yelp.

Great times. But don't let Burkey's mishap put you off. It's a nice descent – technical for sure, but a good test of your skills and not so fast that if you do have a bit of a twitch you won't be able to correct. We're approaching Vico now and the climb to Montecatini Alto. This was one of the first climbs I ever did in Italy, arriving in April after racing the team pursuit at the Track Worlds in Bordeaux. The rest of the boys had been in Quaratta for a few weeks and were acclimatising. I was big and strong and built for four minutes of intense effort, not drags up steep slopes. As I ground my way up here, swinging from side to side, sweat pouring off me, I had plenty of time to appreciate the differing skills and weight of the elite track rider and the elite road racer once again. The climb is only a couple of kilometres long. In fact, these days I wouldn't even consider it a climb compared to the stuff we routinely suck up in the Grand Tours. Back then it reduced me to a chastened silence, which just shows you how everything in the cycling world is relative. When you give them the time and effort, you can conquer things that once conquered you.

We'll hang a left now to pick up the SP40 into Serravalle. You'll know you're on the right road because you'll be able to hear and often see the motorway that runs alongside. One of my all-time favourite climbs is coming our way: the Zoo Climb, named because we'll ride past the Giardino Zoologico di Pistoia on the SP17. Have I ever actually been to the zoo? Add it to the not-yet list along with the Teide cable car and Leonardo's museum – you know me by now – but I love riding past it, and I love the road that takes you onwards. Never too steep, it has many of the same elements that make Pescia such fun: nice sweeping bends, wide and spacious. 7% on a big road always seems much easier than 7% on a narrow one, which makes no sense, but feels good all the same.

As we crest the top, we find ourselves back on the plateau again. There are plenty of water fountains here to refill your bottles, one of the many other lovely touches about riding in this part of the world. Top up, splash a little over your head and neck if it's a warm one, and take the first left turn to start heading down to Marliana on another pleasantly twisty descent. It's steep at times, a tough little climb if you went up Alto and then headed straight here, but it never gets as tight as Burkey's Corner, and you've still got that espresso keeping your brain sharp and your concentration locked, so all will be well.

Mind you, we've had a slight mishap down here as well, back in those early days when everything was new. Max said, 'Take it steady down here, boys – it can get a little tight.' Yeah, okay, Max ... Full gas, down we go, only to meet a van coming up the other way. I managed to just slip past, but my rear wheel was sliding right, trying to catch up with my front, and into the gravel by the side of the road I went, down into the ditch and on to my arse. I looked up to see Max shaking his head. Lesson learnt? Not really ...

It's a lovely pedal on from the bottom back to our old friend, Montecatini Terme. If you're with me, I'll have been talking about the next stop all day long. We used to call it the Cappuccino King. Locals know it as Il Re Del Cappuccino. It's a little place on the corner of a cobbled street called Via Garibaldi. While the original owner has passed away now, his son has taken up his tools to carry his legacy on into the future, and the coffee is nothing short of extraordinary.

The cappuccino is so thick you can almost stand your spoon upright in in. I'm not quite sure how – maybe it's the condensed milk, maybe it's the near miraculous consistency of the foam – but it's so sweet you only ever need one. You might not even require another brioche or *crostata*, that's how good it is. The king is dead, long live the king. (One small side note: drinking a cappuccino after midday is frowned upon in Italy. When you ask an Italian why, the response may not necessarily help. 'It just is ...')

High on the sugar, caffeine charging round the legs, it's back lanes all the way now to Quarrata. I'm going to cut you loose at this point, because you really can't go wrong. Every road is fun. Have a look at your Garmin, check your phone map, plot your own wiggle. Just keep it at a pace you're happy with. In our young and wild days we would often find ourselves drawn into an inadvertent race on these final stretches, sometimes with unintended consequences. Ben Swift was the first to hit the deck on one mad day, Ross Hunter-Reid going over him, landing hard and ending up with a broken wrist.

It ruled Ross out of training for a few weeks, a gap in his life he filled by getting so into *The O.C.* that he managed to finish every series they ever made. You'd wake up in the morning and he'd be watching *The O.C.* You'd get back from your ride and he'd be watching *The O.C.* You'd go to bed at night and he'd still be watching *The O.C.* There would be times when he'd get up from the sofa to go to the bathroom and he'd be watching *The O.C.* on his laptop. Swifty felt terrible when the accident happened. Ross could not have looked more content.

When you return to Quarrata? You'll need food. And, since you're in Italy, your options are many and glorious. If you're starving and after quick gratification, hit Punto Pizza on Via Montalbano. They sell it by the slice and it's the best pizza you'll ever have. You could make a winning return to Bar G, where the *aperitivo* come out around 6 p.m. You can eat your dinner there without even trying to eat dinner. It used to be free, but eventually they cracked on to our ruse and started charging a Euro per person. Brutal.

If you want more? Make your beverage in the G an Aperol spritz, then head for Ristorante Il Cavallino Rosso da Fischio on Via Vecchia Fiorentina I Tronco. This is Tuscany. Embrace the region, its food and its wine. They do a T-bone steak that still reduces me to shivers. Have some nice pizza bread to start, then straight to the T-bone with *pinzimonio* (raw veg) straight out of the back garden on the side and a dip of vinegar and oil, all of it washed down with a lovely local red. It's a special occasion. You're in Quaratta – a great town, a great ride, a great aftermath.

# Bridging the Gap

# End of a Continent

You have time for proper conversations on a long bike ride. Catching up with mates, letting the miles roll by under your tyres and the chat unspool alongside. There's no rush. It can all come out. And by all, I mean the random stuff as well as the obvious: whether you would rather win the Worlds or the Olympic road race; if you would rather be a 60kg rider or an 80kg one; the top three greatest cities to visit in the world.

My answers to those questions? The Worlds, now; 80kg at this stage of my career; and Los Angeles, New York or Copenhagen – and Cape Town.

It's not a hard case to make. I've been to Cape Town three times, and it's one of those rare places that doesn't just live up to your dreamy expectations, growing up as a kid in the Cardiff suburbs, but sprints past them. You've seen all the aerial shots of Table Mountain before you go – the layer of cloud that sits around the top, the steep square sides, the two oceans beyond. You've watched the big rugby matches at Newlands. You've watched the Test matches and one-dayers at the cricket ground just over the road.

Then you get there, and Table Mountain looks even bigger and more impossible, and you abseil down it and realise how high those clouds were, and then you go shark-diving just up the coast and hang around on a cool beach with another great beach round the next headland, and wander down the waterfront and drink the coffee and the wine, and think: there is so much to do here that I could keep coming back every year until retirement and still only be skimming the surface.

It was in my early days in the pro peloton with Barloworld that it first took hold of me. It was an Italian-based team, but with a South African sponsor. I had two South African team-mates in Robbie Hunter and Darryl Impey, both of them from Johannesburg, but when I asked them about Cape Town they raved about it. I was an open door, anyway, and that push sent me down there in November one year. Nothing about it disappointed.

I stayed in Camps Bay, one of those places where it makes no difference where you rent, because you're pretty much guaranteed a sea view everywhere you go. There's a big, wide, sandy beach with houses climbing up the slopes beyond. It can be windy there, and one toe-dip in the sea reminds you quite how far south you are and how comparatively close you are to places that are mainly snow and icebergs. Of course you get in, because that's the rule whenever you go to a beach, whether it's Aberaeron or Auckland or South Africa. None of them are that warm, to be fair. Maybe it's my road-rider's build.

We're starting this ride here, on the beach road in Camps Bay, and we're going east along the M6, the coastal road. We pass Llandudno, which is slightly freaky to a Welshman, but more of that on the return leg. For now appreciate the sights and vibe of Hout Bay – its cafés, its location, its rather handy bike shop. Ben Swift came out here a few years after me, and there's a reason why he started looking at plots of land and talking of grand plans to buy and build.

It's Chapman's Peak that'll first warm our legs. You'll enjoy it: not too testing, a nice gradual gradient of the sort you might find in south Wales. It's right on the coast, rocky cliffs to your left, dropping down to the sea on your right. Nine times out of ten the sun will be shining, even if the air is fresh. It's a toll road for cars and free for bikes, so the tarmac is often all for you and your fellow travellers.

We drop down to Noordhoek and hug the cliffs on your left. To the right is another wide sandy beach, always quiet whether it's peak summer or deeper winter. There will be windsurfers to admire, because the air is seldom still at the southernmost tip of a continent, and there will be surfers bobbing around in the breakers beyond the shore, because the sea has a long way to travel before hitting these southern shores.

It's a busier road for us now. Glencairn Expressway, still technically the M6, but with a good hard shoulder and wide enough lanes. You should be safe from the sometimes questionable driving skills of some of the locals. There aren't as many riders on the road here as in Europe, so drivers don't always seem to expect us. Maybe it's a spatial awareness thing; South Africa is so vast that in most parts you can use as much of the road as you like and it's not an issue. The views remain excellent, nonetheless. We're on the Cape Peninsula, so the sea will be our near-constant companion.

It was around here I once had a double puncture. Only a few months before, Froomey had warned me: just be careful when you stop. Now this wasn't just a South African thing. As a young man in South Wales I was changing a puncture once when two lads walked over to me and asked me a question. The next thing I knew

I was waking up on the ground with no rear wheel to put back in. On this occasion, thousands of miles from home, all was fine. I only had one spare inner tube, so I changed the front and left the back, on the basis that at least I'd have a bit more control with the front pumped up. I began to head back to Chapman's Peak, hoping to see some cyclists. Sure enough, there were plenty, several of whom were happy to give me an inner tube. I think they even changed it for me, said no to my offer of financial compensation and waved me on my way. Totally the opposite experience to Froomey.

At the bottom of a nice descent, turn right at a set of traffic lights. You can stay on the coast at this point and gradually make your way all the way round in a rather cool loop. But we're heading to Redhill on the M66 and another good climb, this one tougher than Chapman's Peak – a little steeper, a little longer, a couple of testing switchbacks.

We pass a township here. Bleary-eyed workers stand in groups by the side of the road in the early hours, waiting to squeeze into the minivans that act as unofficial taxis round these parts. It's a good counterbalance to the wealth we rode past in earlier kilometres. That's the great thing about riding your bike in different places around the world. You take in the smaller roads and therefore, quite naturally, the truer nature of a place. You're slower than a car, so the landscape is only seldom a blur. Should you be on a bad day – legs hurting, lungs burning, motivation struggling – you are kept grounded by all the other things that come your way. Keep your eyes open and there are always reminders of how lucky you are to simply ride your bike for a living.

South Africa has a reputation in some quarters. I'll mention elsewhere the sort of equipment Robbie Hunter used to stash in his back pocket to keep himself safe. On my first trip down here I had Team Sky head mechanic Gary Blem, a native of Pretoria himself, follow me on these roads in a car, just to keep an eye on things. As it turned out, the greater threat to me was the diet I was on to try to shift some excess kilograms and look good before our next team training camp. Meeting Blemski at 7 a.m. I would often have a mere apple in my belly for breakfast. I like apples as much as the next man, but there's a reason I've used the plural there and there's a reason why I don't recommend you do the same, riding these constant undulations and frequent headwinds.

But it's good riding. On all subsequent trips I dispensed with the trailing car. I knew where I was going and I felt perfectly safe. So here, at the top of Redhill, we'll drop back down to the other side to be presented with two equally pleasant options. You can hang a right to head back to Cape Town and save your legs for another day, or go left on Plateau Drive and keep heading further south to Smitswinkel Bay.

Did I say two options? We've just opened up a third. There's a right-hand turn just before you enter Smitswinkel Bay. This is a toll road that takes you all the way down to Cape Point. This one charges those on two wheels as well as four, but it's worth it for the views, the adventure and the sheer braggable nature of it. This is Cape Point Nature Reserve. There's a spectacular lighthouse pretty much on the point where the Atlantic and Indian oceans meet. But more than anything, how many times do you get the chance to ride to the very end of an entire continent?

It's an out-and-back. I feel I shouldn't have to explain that, having just made the comment about the very end of an entire continent, but maybe you live in the very middle of an entire continent. So we're back on the M4, heading north along the eastern side of the peninsula to Simon's Town.

I had a shock when I first rode through here. Penguins! I'd always assumed you had to be on the Antarctic to spot these little charmers, but it seems not. Many years later, on my first trip to New Zealand, I saw some more on the east coast of South Island. Mind blown twice. More prosaically, the cafés here are good, so if you have also endured a mental shock, this is the place to stop. South Africa can be something of a lottery for good coffee, a little like the UK, but you can get lucky and hit Australian standards. However, just when you're relaxing, it can then without warning slip to French levels. In Simon's Town, you're on safe ground.

We can do Redhill twice, now you have fresh energy in the legs. Rather than turning left at the top, drop down and turn right to Scarborough and then on to Misty Cliffs. No great penguin-style shocks here; there are cliffs, and every time I've ridden past them they've been shrouded in mist. It's as if it has its own microclimate, and a spooky one at that. This whole stretch of coastline gets the heart going. It's rugged, beautiful and different to anywhere else I've ridden, except maybe the more *Lord of the Rings* parts of New Zealand.

One thing to warn you about round here. There are always monkeys and baboons running about. Sometimes, when I've ridden through with an emergency banana in my jersey pocket, I've had the nagging sense that they've been eyeing me up. I've never been chased, but I've been smelt. That's how it feels. One time it all became a bit too much. I thought I spotted one beginning to follow me. I'm not proud of it, but I panicked and threw my banana away. The last thing you need on an already testing training ride is a baboon clambering all over your back, tearing at your jersey pockets.

That's Africa for you. We're not in the Vale of Glamorgan any more. With the beauty come the beasts. Another one of the lads was pedalling through here once when he was attacked by a huge bird. His theory was that the bright colours on his helmet set it off somehow. It put the frighteners on me, to the extent that when I was riding with Chris Froome up in Crystal Springs I expected to see lions jogging alongside us every time we entered the countryside. At one point I spotted a massive white thing coming down the road towards us. Holy shit, was my first thought. It's a rare albino lion, was my second. No, it's just a large white cow, was my third.

Scarborough, Misty Cliffs, back to Noordhoek and over Chapman's Peak once more. It's one of those climbs that feels quite different depending on the direction you're taking, so enjoy its reversible charms once more. Drop back down towards Camps Bay and this time appreciate the other Llandudno a little more.

There are some similarities between the two. Both have steep descents down into the bay. Both have sandy beaches. The Welsh one is less frequently sunny; the South African one is better for surfing. The Welsh one has pubs; the one here has no street lights or shops. From this one you can also walk to a nudist beach at Sandy Bay. If there is a nudist spot in north Wales I salute the bravery of all those prepared to go naked in such brisk conditions.

As we climb back out of Llandudno, reflect on one more thing: we have done a decent amount of climbing today so shouldn't we do one more? It's Signal Hill Drive you're looking for, taking us up to Lion's Head. It's not long and it's not hard, but the views are great and there are cafés at the top for that beer you've been thinking about all day. A fitting end to one of my favourite rides in one of my all-time favourite places.

# Adelaide Adventures

Certain places just mean certain seasons. Cardiff, now, is Christmas. July, usually, is some mad lap of France. April and May used to be a high-altitude camp in Tenerife, until it became Granada. And Adelaide? That was always January – training miles, building strength, the Tour Down Under. And while I love the festive period in south Wales, with all the excess and Christmas lights and cosy fireside evenings, there is no better feeling than leaving the heavy grey skies and January blues of the British winter for the impossibly deep blues everywhere you look of the Australian summer.

It's not just more blue, it's a different blue, and it's not just warmth, it's a hairdryer in the face. Which why, when I'm down in Adelaide in the Aussie south, I'd advise you to do what I always do and stay on the coast at Glenelg, where the sand is soft and the cafés outstanding, and the breezes quite the treat when you're struggling with the transition from one hemisphere to the other.

I've never wanted to be one of those old pros who whinges about the attitude of the younger generation of riders. Let's frame this instead as some wise words of advice from an experienced, older head: when it's the start of the year and you're getting your body ready for all that may come in the months ahead, you can enjoy aspects of your day and still be giving your best to training. Of course you could stay in a hotel in the middle of Adelaide and lie on your bed each afternoon, and never venture out into the culture beyond. Or you could stay by the beach, rent yourself a nice apartment with a pool and a barbie, and live a little piece of the Aussie dream. You can still do your rides exactly as your coach advises and you can still work hard and eat well, but you're no more committed to your pro life if you're miserable than if you enjoy a little of your downtime, too.

To our riding. There's a gentle warm-up if you fancy one before breakfast. Get on your bike and ride north at a more leisurely pace on the coast road from Glenelg to Henley Beach. Relax in the knowledge that pretty much every café you come to will have decent coffee, plus eggs and avo, and that you'll have to be really unlucky to get a bad version of either. It's like the opposite to France, where you have to know exactly where you're going and have testimony from at least two independent sources to stand any chance of not getting a stinker.

Awake now, fuelled up and happy, we turn east and head along Anzac Highway, the main road into the city of Adelaide itself. It sounds big and fast and heavy on traffic, but it's doable, the same route the pro teams take on recovery days before the Tour Down Under, when they pedal out from the official race hotel to the seaside and back for a guaranteed good coffee.

There are buses using this road, but there's a bike path on the inside. You'd have to be pretty unlucky to be cut up by a bus turning into a stop, as I was right at the start of my career, here as part of the Barloworld team. There are drivers with chips on their shoulders in Aus. It's a nation that loves its rules. Two abreast on a bike path? Someone will be outraged. A tiny bit outside the bike lane? Someone else will be outraged. Keep your wits about you if you're riding in a group. Smile. Spread the bike love. I was alright about it, on this occasion. No-one got hurt. The driver stopped in plenty of time and apologised.

Less happy about it was my South African team-mate Robbie Hunter, whose character combined all the natural combativity of a sprinter with the natural combativity of a South African and then tripled it because he was Robbie

Hunter. Robbie never was a man to take a backward step. When I joined Barloworld as a callow kid straight off the GB track programme I was genuinely scared of him. I'd heard the stories. If it came to a choice between a bus slamming its brakes on for Robbie or Robbie slamming his brakes on for a bus, the ten-ton lump of metal and rubber would be the one to acquiesce. I remember going into Robbie's hotel room one day and asking him why he was putting an electric shaver in the back pocket of his jersey. That's when he told me it was a taser.

I suppose if you grow up in South Africa you have a different attitude to what might befall you at a set of traffic lights than you do when the most dangerous junction in your world is the turning out of Tesco Extra in Gabalfa on to the A48. Whatever, there's no other way of putting this: Robbie lost his shit with that bus driver on the Anzac Highway, and every time I ride out along it now I remember the moment and feel slightly scared all over again.

We skirt the southern side of the city centre and its shopping streets, leaving the floodlights of the Adelaide Oval cricket ground and the Sir Don Bradman Museum for another day. It's east along Greenhill Road, although you can wiggle and waggle your way however you like, as long as you end up in Magill and on the Magill Road.

Much of Adelaide is built on a grid system, like an American city, so you can never go too wrong as long as you keep counting your rights and lefts.

The B27 is the road that takes you into Adelaide Hills. You can stick to that one if you fancy, but the insiders' option is to hang a left as you leave Magill on to the smaller and much more alluring Norton Summit Road. It's something of a local classic, this one – just under 6.5km at an average gradient of just over 5%, the first chunk of it with great views back down to your left over the city's fringes, the second a sort of false flat, the next a series of very pleasing switchbacks before a last blast up some proper steep stuff.

It's always hot in South Australia. Certainly hot by Welsh standards, but hot by standards in many other parts of Australia, too. However, for all the effort you'll be putting in on the pedals, it is cooler as we ascend into the mountains than it is down below. It can touch 40°C without a problem in the city centre in summertime, so the mid-30s up here can feel like Barry Island by comparison. And thinking of south Wales, as I frequently do, this climb reminds me more of the sort of stuff you get north of Cardiff and into the valleys than it does the big stuff in the south of France. It's interesting, but not too steep; it's long enough for a good workout at this early point in the year without blowing your doors off. There are plenty of trees to shade you from the worst of the sun and, if you fancy throwing an effort or two in, the road will reward you generously.

It's sociable as well. Those who love their road riding in this part of the world – and there are plenty, because the Tour Down Under pleases the hardcore and converts the dabblers – know all about the climb to Norton Summit, and so do the other northern hemisphere pros who choose to winter in Australia. In early 2023 I was riding up here, feeling slightly the worse for a draggy bacterial infection I had, when I saw a guy ahead of me also struggling to find a pleasing pedalling cadence. Turned out it was Łukasz Wiśniowski, the Polish classics man who had been at Team Sky in 2017 and 2018. We enjoyed a most pleasant time telling each other of our woes, and our hopes, and our dreams, and when we waved farewell I think both of us felt much better about it all.

We'll have a good sweat on by the time we reach the summit at Teringie Drive. There are a couple of shops at the top where you can refill your bottles, and I'd make the most of that, for we have plenty of Antipodean adventure still to come. We're back on the B27 now, heading towards the town of Lobethal, via Basket Range, Forest Range and Lenswood, and although it's the main road, it's a nice one – twisty, up and down, not too many cars. You're in the trees at times for a bit of cover and, while the road is bumpy in parts, the surface is generally perfectly acceptable. The only thing you want to watch out for, if you're riding two abreast, is some of the corners. There's a few that are quite sharp and tighten up on you without much warning. I've done team rides there when the younger guys on the front haven't been expecting it, and have ended up bumping shoulders mid-corner. That's never a good thing. Keep your wits about you. Stay upright.

I do love the big Aussie gum trees. Great for shade, and – should you possess the eyes of a hawk, like my old Team Sky team-mate Bernie Eisel – a great place to spot dozing koalas. The downside of having them by the side of the road is how their roots spread out and force up the tarmac. You don't want to hit one of those bumps and lose your hands off the bars. Which reminds me: wear some mitts. You'll be sweating a lot. The last thing you want is hands slipping off the damp bar tape. You can also use them to wipe off the perspiration from your eyes as you climb. Just remember to remove them at the café. We do have our standards.

Time for a change of direction at Lobethal. Having been heading pretty much due east since leaving the beach at

Glenelg, we'll now turn north-westwards towards Cudlee Creek along the eponymous road. Once we're through there it gets spicy again, because when we go left on to the B31 at Millbrook we're on to Gorge Road, one of the true classic stretches of so many Tours Down Under.

We'll often descend Gorge Road in the race, although they've taken us back up it, too. And having done both, I'd have to say it's much nicer to do it in training. When you're racing it, everyone fresh, no-one yet worn down by the slings and arrows of the season, you can end up haring down it at 80 or 90kph, everyone upgrading their front rings to 55 or 56 teeth, flying down like lunatics. The road is good and there's seldom much gravel, but there are a few little kickers in the road, which means riders coming up behind you at sudden pace, and before you know it you're going round corners six abreast and wondering what the hell you're all doing when this is only the first race of many you hope to survive this year.

But wait. Before we hit the really fast bit, we're taking in the best sort of diversion, up right to Paracombe along Torrens Hill Road. The headlines here might scare you like Robbie Hunter on a hangover. Maximum gradient 28%! An average of 8%! But just as I never actually saw Robbie deploy his taser, so this climb is less aggressive than it might be – a mere 1.7km in length, so a challenge and nod to the heritage of the Tour Down Under rather than anything to make you turn tail and head home in defeat.

Pace yourself. That's my advice. It is pretty steep at the bottom, and you do have to attack it, but at the same time it doesn't really ever level off either, so you need to keep a little powder dry. You will appreciate, as you battle on, why it keeps on being included in the Tour Down Under and why it was decisive to Richie Porte's overall win in 2017, as well as to Rohan Dennis when he won the ochre jersey in 2015.

At the top, offer yourself a quiet word of congratulations. Much more than a word might be hard to manage with the lack of air in your lungs, so either throw in that U-ey now and head back down to the turning off Gorge Road, or drop down on Churchett Road to pick it up a little further along. And for all I've said about the speed on this section, you should be fine, partly because you shouldn't have any overly enthusiastic young pros trying to beat you into every corner, and partly because it's all fun as well as fast.

You might get a headwind. You often do, blowing up off the distant coast and funnelling up here. Rather than celebrate its slowing effect, you'll probably bemoan the fact that you're now pedalling on such a rapid descent. If it's not that, it'll be the heat of the wind. Remember the 40°C in the city? You're now hammering back down into it. Remember the hairdryer? It's now on full blast. Told you you'd need that water in your bottle.

If you're on Gorge Road rather than Churchett, you'll pass Kangaroo Creek reservoir on the left as the road swings hard right with the creek also down to your right. Now we'll go left on to another little classic with a special memory for me. This is Corkscrew Road, so named for its tight bends higher up, 3.3km from the turning at the bottom to the church at the top, and with a punchy little average gradient of 7.1%.

I was back in the Team Sky ranks in early 2013 after being part of the team pursuit quartet at the London Olympics the previous summer, and I'd both hung on to some of that track power and also been inspired by what Brad Wiggins had done at the Tour de France just before those Olympics. I knew at this point that road-racing was the future for me, which was one of the reasons I attacked hard on Corkscrew when the second stage of the Tour Down Under came up it.

We were about 5km from the finish line when I made my big move. It did a bit of splintering and, while Movistar's Javier Moreno and Radioshack's Ben Hermans caught up with me on the descent into Campbelltown, I bided my time and hit them hard with my track speed with 400m to go, holding on to win by two seconds. It was quite the boost for me at that stage of my career. I held on to the leader's jersey for three days, finished third in the overall and, in one of my biggest claims to fame, even beat André Griepel to the sprinter's jersey, which certainly hadn't been part of the plan at the start.

Here's what I learned that day a decade ago. It drags up at the start, the road surface heavier than Gorge Road down below. It then drags up a bit more and gets steeper as you ascend towards those hairpins. Go wide on those bends; there are no prizes for trying to be a hero, launching yourself up the inside and potentially not making it round. There are some trees and some shade, but this is all about you and the road. If the thought of Moreno and Hermans on your tail isn't enough to get you up it, think of it this way instead: Corkscrew is the Alpe d'Huez of South Australia. A much smaller one, but still.

At the top, spin your legs. Be grateful you're not racing to a finish line with two rivals arcing towards your rear wheel. Head to Montacute and down Montacute Road. Criticise Aussie map-makers all you like, but they do make navigation nice and straightforward. We're heading south towards Ashton, picking up Marble Hill Road, and we'll take in Mount Lofty (see what you did there, map-makers). This is where the Tour Down Under finished in 2023, coming up the other way from Stirling, and it's a solid little kicker. It also means that our Adelaide Adventure has incorporated three of the summit finishes that have featured in the race in recent years, which is something nice to drop into casual conversation when you get home.

Keep going south on the B28 and you'll come to Cleland Wildlife Park, a good place to meet your family if you're here with them. Think of it as a petting zoo full of creatures that you instinctively don't want to pet: kangaroos, snakes, various scuttly things. Sa and I took Macs here and, while he was understandably cautious at the start, by the end of the afternoon he had joeys quite literally eating out of his hand.

Fill your bottles one more time. From here we're dropping into the town of Stirling, with its excellent cafés. Give the Essence Café on Mount Barker Road a go. I ended up there with Łukasz Wiśniowski, and their banana bread mopped up any remaining moans we had after our ride.

Now it's all about the options. You can head back to Adelaide and Glenelg beyond down the bike path, which runs alongside the highway and is obviously closed to cars. Back into the hairdryer, glad you're by the beach and booked into that apartment with the pool. If you're keen for more, you can tack on an extra loop around Stirling, taking the B33 towards Mylor and hanging a right on Aldgate Valley Road, maybe the nicest road in the entire area. It's not too steep, it's got flowers, it wins awards for its prettiness. Don't say I haven't treated you.

And then there is our third option. Sure, it means another 30-odd kilometres in the saddle. But we're here to ride, aren't we, and if you're in South Australia can you really leave without a trip to the wineries of McLaren Vale?

You can take your pick of vineyards and attendant restaurants round here. Personally, I like Chapel Hill Winery, not least because they let me in despite me only having had a Belgian shower (see page 159) in the back of the rental car Sa had driven her and Macs over in. The roads out there from Mylor are no thrillers – long, straight, flat, not many flowers, frequently a headwind – but you know you will eat and drink of the best when you do get there.

Want one more local delight, just so you can really boast when you get home? We're really not far from Willunga Hill here. I refer you to *Mountains According to G* for the full lowdown, but for now, consider only this: if you could actually complete four big Tour Down Under climbs in one day, why the hell wouldn't you?

# GC Dreaming

# The Guimar Loop

First things first, Guimar is in Tenerife. I've been to Tenerife on more training camps than I can accurately remember, so I've done the Guimar loop a lot and it has a special place in my heart, but I would urge you not to make the same mistake as I did, all those years ago, when I rode it for the first time.

It's a long old pedal, this one, but it's one to savour, like a great book or an epic film. And just as you would no more try to watch the entire Netflix *Tour de France* documentary in a single evening by fast-forwarding as much as possible, so you should let the mileage on this one come to you, rather than chasing it.

There are certainly tougher rides, but this is Tenerife's equivalent to an out-and-back flat ride where the first half takes you an hour with a raging tailwind (and you don't acknowledge the head wind and instead think you're a hero ready to take on the world) and then suddenly you turn round into a block headwind and it's two purgatorial hours home again, and you want to retire and take up golf instead.

For us, staying on the top of Mount Teide, the dormant volcano forming the giant cone that is Tenerife, this ride starts with a descent followed by the flattest road on Tenerife, which is by no means actually flat by the standards of any other land mass, before climbing up 2000m on to a rolling plateau at the top. Here's how the conversation went with my coach at the time, Tim Kerrison, as I saddled up for that first attempt.

'You'll enjoy this one, G. The other boys loved it.'

'How long is it?'

'Just over five hours' riding.'

And here's how the conversation went afterwards.

'How did you find it, G?'

'Good. I did it in four hours fifty-eight.'

'Why?'

'Just thought I'd push a bit.'

'How do you feel?'

'Knackered.'

'It's a long camp, G. Next time ride slower. That's the whole point of Guimar.'

So take your time. This is about mileage in your legs, not smashing out efforts. It's building a base, not bulldozing your legs to pieces.

On our team training camps we stay in the Parador at the top of Mount Teide. For this ride we'll begin in Granadilla de Abona, because unless you're a pro athlete staying at the top for altitude gains, I'm guessing you'll be in the tourist resorts down on the coast. If you are, I'd consider driving up to here. I'm not saying you couldn't ride up from the coast and join the loop. It's not too far in pure mileage terms. I'm just thinking of your legs.

It's a lovely start from Granadilla out along the coast road, if you can call a road that wobbles around between 500m and 700m above sea level a coast road. It's an easy start in terms of directions, too, as we're on to the TF-28, which tracks along the eastern side of the island, parallel to the shore. The extra height keeps the views spectacular, and the heart and lungs working hard.

We go through Cruz de las Animas, El Rio and La Cisnera. It sounds good and it is – never flat, even though we're roughly following the contour lines around the island, up and down and always interesting. You cross bridge after small bridge, some of them more like tunnels to let the winter rain flow down from the heights to the sea. Tim had another trick the first time you rode this loop, which was to ask you to count the bridges you crossed. Most newbies began diligently, stuck to their task as the total went past fifteen and twenty, and then got into a conversation with a team-mate around the thirty-mark and lost count entirely. Even now I'm not sure if it's in the mid-forties or pushes into the fifties.

Give it a go, if you're feeling sharp, but concentrate on the road, too, because it's always twisty and seldom dull. I remember Pete Kennaugh going straight on at one bend when he would have liked to have gone left, and all because we were doing a few through and offs as a group on a road that is too sinuous to sensibly do so. It goes twist-crazy between Arico Viejo and Icor, so watch out for that, but keep your eyes peeled at all times and stay upright for the fun ahead.

And stay on the TF-28 all the way, through Fasnia and El Escobonal, La Medida and Pájara. You'll know it's time for the descent into Guimar when you pass a steep cliff wall to your left and can look down to your right to see the town. It's only a couple of kilometres, but it's a pleasant swoop down. It reminds me a little of the bottom section of the Col du Portet in the Pyrenees, above the town of Saint-Lary-Soulan, when you have the sheer mountain face on your right as you climb and the valley dropping away to your left. There's a big old drop-off here and you don't want to go over it. Scrub your speed before the corners, undercook them rather than overshoot them, and try not to look back over your shoulder at the top of the volcano and consider the fact you'll be climbing all the way back to the top of it before today's riding is done.

Guimar is a good chance to fill your bottles with fluids and your back pockets with snacks. It's a long way to the top now and there are precious few places to stop when out of town. There might actually be nowhere, unless you fancy knocking on someone's door and testing out your Google Translate Spanish.

Leave town on the main road, our old friend the TF-28, and then go left at La Hidalga on to the TF-245. If we're going to do efforts – and our coach has cleared such an approach – we might begin them here. All the way to the top is just under 35km, beginning at 300m above sea level and ending at 2280m, with an average gradient of 5.8%. The quickest I've ridden this section is about an hour and a half, my average power at 375 watts. Within that we might spike every ten minutes or so, simulating an attack in a race or a response to an attack. But only the gung-ho or foolish would attempt a spike in the last half an hour, which is a solid little effort at the best of times. Any time you're riding over 2000m, your body knows about it and you have to adjust accordingly. It'll depend on how good you naturally are at altitude and how acclimatised you might be, but pushing out 380 watts at 2000m takes roughly the same effort as pushing 400 watts at sea level, if not more.

Remember those sums on the way up, but enjoy yourself too, because you're in a beautiful part of a special place, and you're on your bike and about to see what you've got in the locker. You're not going to go wrong with directions: get to Arafo, 2km up the road, turn right at a petrol station on to the F-523 and from there it's pretty much 18km to the next junction you have to think about. It's a lovely road, too, one of the first they re-laid, and it's all in the sun. It's this eastern side of the island that gets the better weather, while the western side gets the rain coming off the long drag across the open Atlantic, hence the holiday resorts for us Brits on the coast down below. If you're feeling strong, you'll be able to continue the climb when we turn left at that junction and kick on to the astronomical observatory, but let's cross that contour when we get to it.

Technically, as I say, this is the F-523. To us it's known as the McLaren climb, because on one occasion on the Guimar loop we arrived at this point to find the road closed. Why, we asked. Because McLaren are here doing some testing, we were told. You can't get up there for at least an hour.

Which is where the delusions of influence kicked in.

Back in those days Tim Kerrison wasn't a fan of stopping. Not for coffees and certainly not for elite level motor-racing teams.

'Right, let me call Dave. He knows someone at McLaren.'

'Yeah, get Dave B to sort it out. Come on, Tim . . .'

There were only two flaws with this plan: firstly that no-one could get hold of Dave; secondly the doubt he could have sorted it anyway. So we rolled around for a while, went down the mountain a few kilometres and then came back up again, and by the time we'd stopped messing around the climb was open again and had a new name.

A word of insider's advice if you do stop here. Altitude can have a strange effect on your body. It can make you pee more and become dehydrated a lot quicker than normal. The air is drier up top too, so you can get chapped lips within a couple of days. It can also mess with your gut, and our regime diet of limited carbohydrates, high protein, high fibre and protein drinks is a tester at the best of times. Full disclosure: come to Tenerife and your entire poo clock can be knocked sideways. They might not adopt that as a tourism slogan, but I've experienced it and it's a fact. There's a couple of storm drains on this climb that I've had a real good look at down the years. I think we all know what I'm trying to say.

The climb. Oh yes. It's a pretty consistent gradient

all the way up. For most of it you're sheltered from the worst of the wind, at least until the last section towards the top. You're never entirely sure of the conditions as you get higher, and I quite like that – sometimes there might be clouds, sometimes a clear sky all the way up, sometimes a spooky mist that shrinks your world and deadens all the sounds. All you might hear is the sudden roar of a motorbike engine as someone on a slightly faster set of two wheels enjoys their own adventure. About halfway up you leave the pine trees behind, but even in direct sunlight it can get cold towards the top, so stick a gilet or light jacket in your pocket to lob on before the descent.

When you reach the junction with the TF-24 – and you really can't miss it – it's a good 14km to the observatory junction. Panic not. You get to the point where you can see the top of the volcano's cone right in front of you, which is always a thrill to a boy from the suburbs of Cardiff. A lot of the time at this point you're also above the clouds, which is another strange sensation when you're from the UK. We're used to looking up at clouds. We're content climbing into them, but it's quite another thing emerging above them, like some high-flying bird or lost drone. No matter how many times I do it, I find it immensely hard not to take a photo. (I refer you to many areas of my Insta feed.)

Even here, on the highest road on the island, it's never flat. You're always either up or down. A few kilometres downhill there's a café, and while you'll fly down towards it (thinner air at altitude, less wind resistance = faster travel), the coffee is terrible and the food not much better. However, when you've climbed as far as we just have, anything tastes good, so if you're going to stop, let me recommend the coffee bom-bom – a heady mix of espresso and condensed milk, the milk sitting all dense and creamy as the bottom layer, the coffee acidic and hot on top. Ride that mighty sugar rush as far as it can carry you.

From the café it's a climb of around 8km to the legendary cable-car that I have never, in all these years, managed to ride. You do have to book ahead if you want to take it and that's why it's not for me; I'm never quite organised enough. You might not fancy it either after such a long ride, but if you do, or you're meeting your family and need to share at least one element of the day's adventuring with them, it takes you right up to 3500m and spectacular views right across all the Canary Islands.

You've done the hard work now. It's just a case of keeping the old spidey senses on alert for a little longer, because the tourists getting out of their cars or walking along the edge of the road tend not to be expecting fast-moving, sugar-rushing cyclists, and may stroll foolishly into the middle of the road to take selfies or moody shots of weird plants that favour ancient lava fields. There will be tourist-filled coaches, too, crawling round bends or exiting into the middle of the road. There was one time in the old Team Sky days when Chris Froome was doing me a favour, filming me with a GoPro camera in one hand for a BBC Wales documentary, his left hand on his brakes, only for a car in front to slam its brakes on for a volcanic-based photo opportunity, and Froomey to go straight into the back of him.

It's pretty much downhill all the way from here back to Granadilla. You'll pass the vast rolling lava fields on your right, where previous eruptions of Teide have splashed their own dark decorations. Cruise the one final kick of a 3km climb, which will either be nothing after what you've done or the end of you, depending on whether you listened to my advice earlier. Then it really is just downhill all the way on the same lovely smooth road 12km to Vilaflor.

But don't get complacent or over-confident on this final plummet. You'll have a good five hours, quite possibly a lot more, in your legs by now, so your concentration levels may be sub-maximal. In Vilaflor you'll come to the confluence of three roads running back down the hills. The first turn-off right is to La Camella, the one place name on the island that makes me smile and shudder at the same time. Smile, as it's a great snake of a name that just rolls off the tongue; shudder as the only time we spoke about it was on an all-out efforts day, with all the pain that brought. The middle road? That's to San Miguel. Unfortunately, nothing to do with the cold beer, just a steep inconsistent bastard of a climb.

The third, which we are taking down to Grenadilla, is the TF-21. It's a lovely smooth road now they've invested in the road surfaces on the island and eliminated the bumpfest of earlier years, with the influx of pro riders and amateurs hunting the same good times. It's twisty in a good way, not as steep as some of the descents on the island and with a nice mix of corners, some tight and technical, others sweeping and fast.

One more potential hazard to flag: you will get a few loose rocks on some of the corners and, depending on the time of year, sometimes some big old acorns from the oak trees all around. I saw Ben Swift have a horrible tumble there once, taking his eyes off the road to grab something from his back pockets, hitting a rock and then the deck, ripping his top open and rupturing his spleen. Ten days in hospital is no way to conclude your holiday. Don't be scared, but do pay attention. Most of the time they do clear the roads, because they appreciate us riders out here.

And then we're back where we began, ideally in more than four hours fifty-eight minutes, usually with a big grin on our faces. Get on to the terrace of a restaurant, take off your helmet, let the Canarian sun dry your sweaty brow and your jersey. It's time for lunch or dinner or whatever you fancy recovering with. Today we have ridden, and we have ridden well.

# Monaco Form-finder

There is a rivalry in professional bike racing between those who base themselves in Monaco and those who base themselves in Andorra. It usually goes a bit like this: the roads we ride are quieter/easier on the eye/nastier on the legs than yours, plus the weather is better here and family life is so good – there's so much to do, mate . . .

Of course, there is no real argument about it. The climate in the south of France is better all year round. Fact. It's also not a three-hour drive from the nearest airport. Sure, you get nice Andorran days in summer, but unless skiing is part of your prep, are you prepared to put up with the other eight months? So when you ride this route, appreciate that it will almost certainly be under clear skies in a pleasant ambient temperature, and spare a thought for those over in the Pyrenees who will be donning rain jackets and thinking about cutting their ride short for a miserable extra hour on the turbo trainer.

Sure, it can get busy on the roads in the south of France in the summer months, so do watch out when overtaking cars or turning left from the right-hand side of the road. There are plenty of tourists about, and they're the ones who will be stressed, not really paying attention and more concerned about looking at the views. They certainly won't be using their indicators. Even so, you'll love this loop.

It was given the name Monaco Form-finder by the Aussie riders based here back in the day: Brad McGhee, who wore the yellow jersey at the Tour and the pink jersey at the Giro; and Stuart O'Grady, who rode in yellow on multiple days and also won Paris-Roubaix. The name will become self-explanatory as you progress around. Much like your classic Aussie, there is no pretending to be better than you are on the Form-finder, and no acting like you're a legend when actually you might be on a bang-average day.

Here's how it works. Head out of Monaco on the Cap d'Ail side, towards Nice. This is the busiest of roads down here – the base corniche, the coast road – but it's still perfectly safe for those of us on bikes, and we're only on it for a couple of kilometres. Then you'll start climbing, because climbing is inevitable when you're leaving the beach for the mountains. It's not brutal, though, what the maps tell you is called Avenue du Maréchal de Lattre de Tassigny and what us Ineos riders refer to as the Polska climb, because it's where our Polish team-mate Michal Kwiatkowski lives. You pass a little bowls club on the way up; if you're coming up later in the day you'll see the old boys of this part of town playing boule, although if you're an early bird they'll be sleeping off the pastis hangovers. I've always secretly fancied dipping a toe into that sort of lifestyle: getting all my training done by early afternoon, then, once fed and watered, kicking back with a personalised set of boule and attendant yellow duster. I'll make the trip up there soon to find out about the membership requirements, joining fee and initiation rites.

The incline is gradual, the road surface good. In the south of France the roads are usually nice and smooth, which I've heard is a contrast to those in Andorra, but that's a discussion for another time. It's twisty, but that simply gives you the opportunity to appreciate the views down to the Côte d'Azur from a number of different directions. Can you see the sea from Andorra? Maybe with binoculars on a clear day – if you're prepared to wait for one.

At the top of the climb you join the Moyenne Corniche,

or D6007 to give it its more prosaic name. It's the middle road, basically. You have the coast road, then this one, which will take you into Èze village if you stick with it, although we're going to turn right and head up towards the outskirts of La Turbie. It was at this junction that I first met Tao Geoghegan Hart, in the days when he was a junior. All his rich talent was already there to see. He was riding up with Ian Stannard. As they arrived, Tao looked fresh and ready for a four-hour roll in the hills. Stannard, eight years his senior and with all manner of pro races behind him, looked like he'd just jumped in the shower for a couple of minutes while holding his breath.

All these roads around La Turbie and Èze have a story to tell. Some are familiar to us from editions of Paris-Nice, otherwise known as the Race for the Sun, and once we're up and away from the coast it always brings back memories of the 2015 edition when Richie Porte and I both crashed on the wet roads while on tyres pumped up so hard we could have raced the team pursuit on the track. That's the problem with Paris-Nice – they tell you you're racing to the sun, and neglect to mention that you're going to pass under some significant rain clouds on the way there.

Your legs will be working now, the blood pumping hard. My father-in-law Eif came out to visit us a while ago and decided he fancied a quick spin up here. It's usually half an hour tops to La Turbie, but that day with Eif it ended up being a two-hour ride. Until that point he had always enjoyed taking the mickey out of my climbing skills. You look like you're going backwards on climbs – that sort of thing. Why don't you try harder, Ger? You get the picture. Safe to say he changed his mind at La Turbie. I've not heard a climbing-related squeak out of him since.

Now, you're going to need food for this loop. If you haven't packed your jersey pockets already, there's a new bakery in La Turbie that can sort you out. It would be too early for a café stop for the hard-as-nails likes of Brad and Stuey, but these rides are for everyone, so if you fancy a coffee and sugary boost then you go for it. You're looking for Ma Première Boulangerie on Avenue de la Victoire. They do a mean chocolate croissant, where the little touch is that the chocolate inside is a very generous portion of Nutella. It's also a good place for lunch on the way back from a ride. I've had the club sandwich and it was massive, and even if food does taste better when you're tired, I'm struggling to think of a better one I've consumed. There is generally a queue, especially at weekends, but it's definitely worth it, and they rattle through the orders, so you shouldn't be waiting too long.

Back on your bike, continue climbing along the D53

towards Saint-Martin de Peille, heading left out of La Turbie. You'll know if you've missed it as the road will start to go downhill and we still need to go up. You then stay on this road all the way to Peille. Sounds complicated? It's actually simple enough. Just make sure you don't go straight on at the first hairpin. If you do end up taking a wrong turn you'll know pretty soon, as you'll probably end up at Monte Carlo Golf Club, which is every bit as swish as you'd imagine. I've been invited to play there on a couple of occasions, but since my last golfing action was the pitch and putt in Heath Park in Cardiff, aged nine, I have reservations about how big a step up it might be.

When I do take the turn on the hairpin, it's hard for me not to wince. This is the exact spot where I crashed in that edition of Paris-Nice, and I still feel slightly cheated. I was in a group of five, the rain smashing down, and the rest of them all came hammering into the corner way too hot. I backed off, being sensible, knowing the local roads. They all overshot it, went wide, got really lucky on the exit and stayed upright. I went in nice and steady, stayed on the inside to give myself plenty of room for manoeuvre, and then slipped on whatever combination of water and wash-off had pooled there. Knowing that corner intimately didn't really help me that day.

So on we ride, and with luck the dramas are behind us for a little while. There's a plateau of about 8km or so as you come round the back of the famous Madone climb and then you're into Peille, still on the D53, ready to start the long descent into Paravieille. It's a nice one, but it's one to concentrate on, not to chat to your mates or try to set a new maximum speed PB. Some descents you can get into a lovely rhythm as you come down, with every corner feeling like a mirror image of the one that precedes it. Here you have some nice, long, wide sweepers, some that tighten up on the entrance and some that tighten up suddenly on the exit. It's not the widest of roads and you do get cars coming up the other way, so you don't want to be over-shooting any blind turns. But it's good fun. Enjoy the feel of the cooling wind on your face.

If you're doing this in winter, be prepared to get cooler still. Once you're over the first set of hills by La Turbie, the temperature generally drops by five or ten degrees anyway – the height gain, the shade, the distance from the sea – just as in the summer months it tends to be the opposite. When you're almost at the bottom of the road here, you'll pass over a small bridge and turn ninety degrees right. It's nothing special to look at, just your average corner, but in the winter months I'm certain it's the coldest spot on the entire Riviera.

It's unbelievable. I have no idea why, but it has its own 10m-long microclimate, and that climate is from the Antarctic. Or Andorra.

You can warm up with the long drag through the next valley all the way up to L'Escarène. Should the cold have got into your bones, there's an extra loop you can tack on here that takes you up to a quarry. It's a mere kilometre in length but pretty steep at the bottom, and quite slippery under your wheels from the shiny clay deposits and the debris from the trucks that carry it all away. There's even a small tunnel at the very top, almost like a half-pipe. Plenty of the boys have tried riding up its wall and back again, thinking they're Tony Hawk or Danny MacAskill rather than skinny men with skinnier tyres.

This extra loop can also come in handy as the usual way up the valley can be blocked by a big metal gate across the road. Generally it's closed before midday every Tuesday and Thursday, so keep an eye on your calendar. I rode it once with Chris Froome and we climbed over the gate to discover five massive machines grinding away at the cliff, spitting out noise and dirt and a general sense of menace. Froomey, maybe there's a reason they've closed this off today . . .

It's only a short blast to L'Escarène. On a hot day – the sort of pleasant heat you only rarely get in Andorra –

you might want to refill your water bottles here. There's a bakery in town where we used to stop quite a lot until we realised that the people who ran it often seemed to be grumpy, as if they had a chip on their shoulder about the modest consumption of road racers in season. I'd move on and use the small Casino corner-shop instead if you want drinks or chocolate. If you're just after water there's a free fountain right next to the shop – a lovely communal touch.

Out of town, and on to the D2204 to Touët-de-L'Escarène and Saint-Laurent. We're on our way to the Col de Braus, a spectacular climb of the sort that looks like a child has zigzagged a marker pen down the mountain. There are two ways to approach it: the long one, where you turn left on to the D2566 through Luceram and then the D21 and D54, and the more usual route which sticks to the slightly bigger road.

The long one is a nice climb, steady at the start but increasingly punchy. I told you you'd find out about your form. Should this be winter, you'll be noticing the snow on the ground more and more as you get out here. When it starts to fall, enjoy it. When it starts to settle, think about dropping back down. Also be grateful you're not in Andorra, where at this point you'd need a shovel and crampons. Richie and I were caught out here once, but luckily we had the team car behind us carrying extra layers of clothing.

I'm guessing you might not be as fortunate, although you may be joined at this point by a number of sports cars going incredibly fast. Maybe because we're out in the back of beyond, maybe because the road twists and turns, but the owners of Porsches and Ferraris seem to enjoy racing round here. If they come up on you fast, and you're riding two abreast and they have to briefly slow down, they never look too happy about it. It is, however, quite cool hearing the roar of their engines through the valley as they get closer, the skips and the spits from those huge engines, the way the whining sound bounces off the mountains all around.

I'd recommend the normal route to the top of Braus. It's not too steep, around 6 or 7%, and it's pretty consistent. The hairpins kick in with 2 or 3km to go and you're always in the sun. We use the climb for training efforts quite a lot, often before the Tour to spark our legs into maximum life. It was here that my former Sky and Ineos team-mate Wout Pouls had something of an altercation with an amateur rider who insisted on sitting on his wheel whenever he could. Wout is an equitable sort, but he was annoyed this guy was following him, and then more annoyed when he started an effort and still couldn't drop him. Two weeks out from the Tour a scenario like this is never good for a rider's morale, no matter how hard the effort. A couple of hours later, ride done, hurt still visible on his face, Wout started getting it in the neck from the same bloke on social media. He still struggled to shrug him off. Hey man, I'm only trying to do my job . . .

At the top of Braus there's also a café, but it never seems to be open. I've lived down in this area over ten years and I think I've seen them in action maybe twice. It's a strange one, the opening times apparently totally random. Next time I'm up there I'll check and keep you posted. It's a great descent off the Braus, dropping down into Sospel, still on the D2204. It's been re-tarmacked a few times, this road, which is no bad thing. I hit a rogue lip of tarmac once, found myself with my hands off the bars in the middle of the road and only just stayed up. Good adrenaline rush though.

We have three options now: really find your form, back off a fraction and let the form come to you, or leg it for home. If it's the last of these you're after, turn right on to the D54 halfway down Braus, ride along the ridge into Castillon, and drop back into Menton and home to Monaco. For the second option – what we might call the Mini Form-finder – continue down into Sospel, where there'll be the final climb of the day waiting for you. It's about fifteen minutes for me if I'm riding hard, but it's nice – through the trees, shaded, twisty enough to be interesting. You do often think you're closer to the top than you actually are, because you can see the triangular mountain peak up to your right and it always seems almost within reach. Watch out for a sign for a tunnel, because that's when you know you're nearly there. One more random crash memory for you: Mark Cavendish's old lead-out man, Mark Renshaw, hit the deck as we descended here. There's nothing worse than crashing in training, especially from just going a little too fast.

The third option, and full Form-finder loop, is to carry straight on through Sospel and on to a longer climb, which will take you up and down into Breil-sur-Roya. There's another fresh water fountain at the top, which is always handy; Sospel's a good place to refuel, now you've opted to go longer. We still have a fair distance to cover, you've got some miles in your legs by now and there's something about small French towns like this: the food, or at least the baguette-shaped food, is very good while the coffee is generally very poor. When I think of Sospel my mind inevitably drifts back to a baguette I had there once that must have been over a foot long. It came accompanied by a plate of chips, just in case you felt cheated of basic carbs. That was some feed. It must have been winter and a long way from any race. Surely?

Back to the big loop. We're still on the D2204, heading to Breil-sur-Roya. The first third of the climb seems rougher, the vibe bringing back memories of the bottom of Rhigos, back home in south Wales. The middle third is flatter. You can use it to recover from what you've done or simply go faster to boost your average speed, depending how your form is. The last third picks up again, but that's all okay – you're nearly there, plus there are a couple of fun hairpins and good views from the very top.

There's a great flow to the descent into Breil; it's not irregular like Peille. You'll sometimes get cars behind you, beeping because they think you're holding them up. You'll also get held up yourself by German tourists on massive motorbikes who are nervous on steep downs or can't quite muscle their big touring bikes round the tight bends. It's a mixed bag of everything, and that's just fine.

Then on to the valley road, and down over the border into Italy at Fanghetto. When I first moved to Monaco, I always found it strange how you could ride in France and Italy during the same training ride, and that when you did so, the roads, culture and everything else changed instantly. You don't need a sign to tell you that you're in Italy. It's obvious – from the holes in the road and the style of the buildings to the drinkability of the coffee.

Seven kilometres over the border there's a great café on the left which we refer to as the Petrol Pump Caff. You'll realise why when you see it. The official name is Bar Gasolina (I refer you to my previous comment). My Ineos team-mate Salvatore Puccio knows the guy who runs it and as a result the owner's always really good to us. Pile in there after the Tour and he'll bring out mountains of food: cheeses, plates of meat, cheese and meat pizzas.

The coffee is decent, the sandwiches are unreal. The cigarettes are clearly cheap, bearing in mind how many French people you see in there buying fags. Even if it's only the coffee and sandwiches you're after, if he's seen you on the telly climbing Alpe d'Huez you'll have cold beers put in front of you and an Aperol Spritz placed next to it. Mainly because of this generous attitude, we've had a few long lunches there, despite how long the ride home still is.

As you wobble off, stomach pushing your bib-shorts out slightly more obviously than before, there are a couple of tunnels to negotiate. They're safe enough – obviously dark, but sufficiently downhill that you shouldn't be taken by surprise by any smoking Frenchmen looking to get back home at pace. If you're scared of the dark, there's a gravel road just to one side that takes you past them.

Job done. And we're sort of done too, in that we're on our way home. The SS20 brings you out into Ventimiglia, and from there you can ride all the way along the coast back to the start. From Venti to Menton, just back across the French border and then to Monaco, is a lot nicer on the bike than going on the busy route from Nice to Antibes and Cannes. Coming this way, from the east, you can see Monaco approaching as you curve round the coast with the sea to your left, which is pretty cool, especially the first time you ride it.

Still peckish? We've got you. If you've taken the shortcut from the Braus via Castillon, or up the Renshaw descent, at the bottom of the road from Castillon to Menton is a decent bakery. Richie Porte used to go there for his quiche, and that's quite the recommendation. Even as a non-quiche man I had to admit that the quiche there is good quiche. If you're a sweet-toothed rider, the lemon meringue quiche (is that even a quiche? I'm out of my depth) is even better. The coffee, since we're now back in France, is once again bang average.

There's another café just up the road which gets the balance right: in France, run by Italians. I go in there wondering which language I should speak, say 'focaccia sandwich' while pointing at the focaccia sandwiches, and then remember that the only language I'm fluent in is

English. They're nice people in there. I've eaten one of their focaccia sandwiches and only realised afterwards that I'd forgotten to bring any money, and they were fine about it. Come back tomorrow – we'll get you a focaccia sandwich ready!

This is also the café where I got my bike nicked. Usually we sit outside and keep an eye on our gear, but this was a cold day. When we came outside my Pinarello had gone. I'd been in an Uber home for about five minutes when I got a call on my mobile.

'Mr Thomas, it's the police in Monaco. We have news of your bike.'

'Wow, that was quick. I haven't even reported it stolen yet . . . '

Turns out three coppers in a riot van had been driving around Menton, bored, when they saw a fifteen-year-old kid on a Pinarello. Quite young to be on a £9,000 bike, they thought. Unusual to be riding something like that without a helmet, or Lycra, in trainers. Doesn't look much like an Ineos rider either, unless their youth programme has gone into overdrive.

I drove back to Menton. Couldn't find the police station, saw a police van and asked the three blokes inside for directions.

'Thomas! We have your bike!'

I jumped in the back, they stuck the blue lights and sirens on. A minute later we're at the police station, I've got my bike and we're all posing for a nice series of selfies.

It's not always so easy being a pro rider in Menton. When it's early summer and your big target race is still ahead, and you're tired and hungry, and pedalling past all these restaurants with people outside on the cocktails, chips being brought out, ice-creams with a minimum of three boules per person, you can get pretty jealous at that point.

You know, too, that all the sacrifices are worth it in the end. Even if that big race turns to shit, you know you've done everything you could and given yourself the best chance to perform as well as possible. And you know from experience that the time will come, in just a few short months, when you can be one of those people in the cafe. One year, after the Tour, my mates Rob and Dale came out to stay with us. We did this loop (the shortest version – they had no form and no interest in finding it either). So we did the cut-off from Braus to Castillon, absolutely screwed, and stopped off in Menton for an Aperol Spritz and lunch.

After lunch, getting our heads around the 20-minute ride home felt like getting up for another three-hour ride. And then, two minutes into the ride home, we turned on to the beach front and were awed by the beautiful blue sky and even bluer sea. Sod it. 'Boys, who's up for a quick dip?'

We took our bikes over the pebbles to the shoreline, left them there and ran into the sea. When we finally got back on our bikes and rode back to Monaco, we stopped at the Italian gelateria in the port and brought our insides to the same cool temperature as our outsides. It might be one of the best rides I've ever done.

# Masca Marvel

For a small island with not many roads and one very big dormant volcano, you can have a lot of fun with your bike on Tenerife. Let's just make one thing clear. When I say fun, I'm talking about the sort of pleasure that we all understand when we ride bikes – pleasure as other people would understand it, and pleasure other people might well interpret as pain.

It's basic science. When you go down, you have to come back up again. But let's be positive: if you go up, you get to come down again. So, as we turn right out of Parador de Cañadas del Teide, the hotel right at the toppermost point of the island where most of the pro teams stay, just bear that in mind. We're going to have a great ride today, but significant elements of the enjoyment will be experienced in the weary yet satisfied aftermath as much as in the moment itself.

It's a draggy little start, but only a brief one, then straight into a 3km climb and a gain of 200m. It's never steep, not properly steep; this first part is often a recovery ride on an Ineos training camp, dropping down towards the cafés for a substandard Canarian coffee. Today we push on further, sticking to the TF-21, and our early reward on the road to La Orotava on the northern coast is probably the single most enjoyable descent on the entire island.

It's smooth, really smooth. You're far less likely to come across a loose stone in the middle of the road than you are on the descent the other way to Guimar, and the views ahead are epic. The weather on this side of the island is more humid than in the south or east, so you're a touch more likely to experience rain on the way down, but it's still only a slim chance and on the clear days you feel like you can see forever.

There is one pitfall to this. Every other tourist on this road will also be keen to stop at the viewing points, so keep your eyes open for slowly reversing coaches and hire cars with burned-out clutches. It's also a road popular with motorbike riders on sunny weekends, for all the same reasons we enjoy it. When you're fizzing round the nice wide corners and picking up excellent amounts of speed, do consider that a motorbike capable of going significantly faster uphill and braking significantly more effectively going downhill might be on your shoulder or coming rapidly the other way. Ian Stannard was cornering in the middle of one of these bends once when he almost had his head taken off by a motorbike doing the same in the opposite direction. It won't happen to you, but just consider it might.

Coming down this road always reminds me of the freakish year when we did so in heavy snow. You don't expect snow in Tenerife. You don't usually ride in it, unless you've been brought up in the sort of places where as a kid the mere sight of it falling from the skies made you excited, which may be why Wout Pouls (who is from the Netherlands) and I both decided to do our ride as planned, and Chris Froome (who grew up in Nairobi) decided to put himself through a hellishly long indoor session on the turbo trainer instead.

We did four hours in the end, with a couple of efforts. It wasn't warm. We had to stop frequently to get extra clothes from our coach Tim Kerrison, following in the team car, and then dry clothes and then extra dry clothes. But we did it, and when we returned to the hotel, red of cheek and frozen of finger if also smug of outlook, Froomey was stricken with a severe attack of the guilts.

That's the way it is when you're a multiple Grand Tour winner. You don't win four Tours de France, two Vueltas and a Giro by taking it easy when others are not. Pausing only to stock the team car with the remainder of his extra dry kit, Froomey headed out into the mayhem and clocked up a further three hours before limping his way back home, broken but finally clear of conscience. However, he wasn't the one who suffered the most that day. By the time Tim returned, he had done about eight hours of driving at 25kph in horrific conditions while other motorists beeped him angrily for holding them up, his hazard lights on for the entirety.

Anyway. We head west just before we hit La Orotava, first along the TF-326 at Chasna and then the TF-324 at Los Realejos. Eventually we'll pick up the TF-342. I have to be honest with you: all the real hurt is yet to come. But, since we've been heading downhill pretty much since that initial short rise, you knew that anyway. Way in the distance is Buenavista del Norte, on the TF-42, down at sea level, but it's a long coastal road, higher up for most of its length than the one we did on the Guimar loop, and a fair bit more up and down too.

There are sections as you pass through the small villages en route that have some pretty steep, if short, climbs and descents, A few sections are quite sketchy. There is one stretch you'll recognise where the tarmac becomes concrete slabs, a deep groove cut through the middle of the road to drain rainwater away. It goes without saying that this is not the place to attempt your new descending speed PB. I should also warn you that when you get to a place called Garachico, you should expect a climb out of it that is twisty, then zig-zaggy, then just plain nasty. It's not the steepest road in the world (Tim Kerrison found that for us, and it's over between the North Airport and La Orotava) but it's still pretty lively.

If you do want to take on the steepest road, it's called Calle Monroy. It's almost worse riding down it than riding up it, because the gradient is so insane in places that you think you're going to fall over your handlebars, even with your backside hanging off the back of the saddle. Also, before you give it a go, please consider these stats: it's 2km in length with an average gradient of 26% and more than 500m of vertical height. It took Tim twenty-four minutes to get up it and Tim's pretty fit. To make that quite clear, it took a fit man twenty-four minutes to ride 2km. End of public service announcement.

The part of the island we're now in feels a bit different. It's more residential; there are fewer holiday apartments. It's a little more of the real Tenerife. That cloudier weather means the landscape looks greener too, almost like a rain-forest in parts, as if you're riding through Colombia instead of the Canaries. The other side is like southern Spain: burned out by the sun in comparison, all yellows and oranges and browns rather than fifty shades of green.

There's wildlife over here – proper wildlife. We spotted a wild boar wandering onto the verge once, which put extra cadence into our pedal stroke. There's always chickens, clucking their way into the road and then clucking off at twice the pace when they spot us coming down the road towards them, and there used to be a chicken man, who would be roasting them on an open barbecue outside his house. One noseful of that aroma and you were desperate to stop. Alas, it was always too early in the ride or too late in the season. I try not to have too many regrets, but never sampling the wares of the chicken man is one of them.

We have an option, when we eventually reach Buenavista del Norte. Most of the time we turn left, which will take us south and into the meat of the climbs. Should you fancy an additional adventure, head on instead, along the TF-445 towards Punta del Teno.

This the most westerly point on the entire island. You have to work to get there, through a long tunnel, pitch black, with absolutely no idea of what might be coming your way. We had to use the lights on our phones when we did it, crawling along at 10kph, wondering what the hell we were doing, and then we emerged blinking into the light and it was all very pleasant. There's a red-and-white striped lighthouse, a few tourists and the satisfaction of having reached the very edge of Tenerife, when the road network doesn't really allow you to ride a complete lap of it. I mean, I wouldn't go back. I feel like I've ticked that box. But you should try it. It'll be better with bike lights; if you don't have those, just make sure your phone is fully charged.

I probably should have mentioned that it's worth refilling your water bottles in Buenavista del Norte, because the real work is about to begin. We turn onto the TF-436 towards El Palmar, which will take us onto the Bananaman Climb. This is not the same as the Banana Climb, for reasons that are about to become clear. The Bananaman Climb is so named for a simple reason: we were riding up here once when we were passed by a guy in a pick-up truck with about 200 bunches of bananas in the back. Perhaps stereotyping the diet of elite athletes, he stopped and gave us a fistful each, completely free of charge. How could we not re-name the road in his honour?

It's a bit steep at the bottom, if I'm honest. You can get a real sweat on here, low down and in the humidity of this side of the island. It's fairly long, too, almost 13km in total, but on the upside there is always something going on, always something to distract you – a couple of nice hairpins, a steady gradient, a local handing out free fruit. It flattens out towards the top, takes you into some trees and under cover, and then rolls on for a bit in more benign fashion. Once you reach the top you'll get to the windiest corner I've ever been around. Nine times out of ten it's blowing a gale straight at you. It's not quite Gent-Wevelgem 2015, when you might recall big men being blown into ditches and me being blown into a flying karate-kick pose, but it's pretty close.

Drop down a couple of kilometres and back up the other side to the viewpoint over Masca. There's a good café here, with great vistas of the *Jurassic Park* landscape and Masca itself. In fact, these few kilometres might just be among the best in this entire book, although some of the technically hardest as well. As the road drops down, it hugs the side of the mountain. It's beautiful and testing at the same time. As the descent continues it becomes steeper and twistier still. It's all fun, of course, in the definition I referred to at the start, but it's not all that wide and the tourists coming up are often on the point of being freaked out by it all, so take it steady. Maybe they're just keeping their eyes peeled for a rogue velociraptor.

The town of Masca is the first you come to as the road flattens up. For a place that's given its name to the ride, I've never actually stopped there for longer than it takes to remove the jacket I put on to keep me warm as I plummeted from the previous summit. At this point thoughts are all of what is still to come, specifically a 3km ramp at an average of 10%. Clearly that's a tester, but imagine what it was like before they resurfaced it, when the road was so rough and bumpy it was like trying to ride up thick sandpaper.

One insider's tip: it's worth starting this ride early in your day, so you can reach this climb before it hits peak tourist coach rush-hour, and enjoy that lovely smooth new tarmac under your wheels, the views that unfurl around you and the clean air that clears with every metre you ascend.

We've had a few coffee stops here, around 500m from the top. However, there's no café, just a nice flat area among the bushes, where you can look out over the jagged cliffs and to the sea.

The coffee stops arose in Covid times, and Tim loved them. He would drive ahead of us to get his camping stove fired up and the coffee brewing. He would also normally make an omelette for himself and the mechanic as well, or fry up a massive black sausage, which I interpreted as a Tenerifian black pudding. I was never jealous of that, to be fair, but these stops were great. Some of the coffee connoisseurs on the team would hand-grind beans, some deck chairs would come out of the car, and we'd park ourselves around a random bush and enjoy the views. Forget all the complications. That's what life's all about.

At the top you'll ride past what looks like a Spanish burger van. Don't get your hopes up. It does pastries instead and, as as a man who doesn't naturally favour the pastry, they've never looked good – dry, flaky and massive. I've yet to be tempted, instead always heading straight on to the next twisty, steep but enjoyable descent.

We're into Santiago del Teide now. Although we've all attempted plenty of coffee stops here, it's never delivered for us. One of the options is a biker café where part of the vibe seems to be making their beverages and the cups they serve them in as average as possible. There is a slightly better option about 100m up the road on the right, where the owner once gave us a load of free empanadas and arepa, the Columbian maize flour thing stuffed with beans and cheese. Perhaps he was related to the Bananaman. The food is good and the opportunity to fill your water bottles open, so I'd dive in.

Sated, replenished, follow the TF-375 towards Guia de Isora and the Bumpy Climb. Readers of *Mountains According To G* will know that Bumpy is no longer actually bumpy, owing to the comprehensive nature of the island's road programme, but it was at the start, so it shall be for ever more. And of all the climbs on Tenerife,

I must have ridden up this one more than any other. I'll do the sums: 11 training camps, each for approximately two weeks, with a minimum of five times up Bumpy each time . . . I'd say it must be close to fifty ascents.

It's usually a team effort up here, replicating what we do on big hilly stages. Riders rotate on the front of the group, holding the pace, setting the tempo. Each man is designated to take us to a certain point and then pull off, taking the team leader on the road all the way to the top at 2,100m. It's very Tour, very Giro – sometimes two of us left at the end, racing for the summit, sprinting the final half a kilometre; sometimes solo, time-trialling it as far as your body and mind will take you. Maybe half the time the leader might not even make it, or the team blows to pieces at some point, generally at the start of the camp when everyone is overly keen, but that's what these efforts are about – communication and good decisions as much as the physical effort. Plenty of riders have lost their rags during these efforts, but that's for another book.

We're in the lava fields again at the top, and the strangeness and the beauty of it can help take your mind off the privations you're putting yourself through. If you're on your own, you'll enjoy the section through the trees lower down, although this is something of a monster when tackled without assistance. If you have your phone and your headphones and can be alert while using both, consider downloading a few episodes of your favourite podcast – perhaps the highly recommended *Geraint Thomas Cycling Club*. Do it before you leave the hotel wifi too, as you'll be out of phone reception for most of the climb.

There's a great view of the volcano as you ascend, although it is something of a tease. When you're the size of Teide, you tend to look closer than you actually are. Two stories of my former Belarusian team-mate Vasil Kiryienka to amuse you as you grind your way up. Kiry was a hard bastard, no two ways about it. On one occasion we were descending this way, the weather worsening with every minute, although the forecast was actually okay. 'In the car it says it's still five degrees,' Tim informed us, which is not the best thing to say to four frozen, wet bike riders.

'Get lower down and it'll be clear – you'll be warm and dry,' he continued, but Kiry wouldn't accept it. As we freewheeled through the sleet, icy water soaking our jackets and running down our necks, he slammed on the brakes and refused to go any further. Even as we tried to reason with him, and then take the mickey, he turned around and headed back to the hotel. Trouble was, the forecast was bang on. While we froze for a while, it was fine at the bottom. Wout, Froomey and I did our efforts, took off our extra layers as we warmed up and then rode back up, feeling great about ourselves and possibly slightly smug.

Two days later Kiry blew up badly on this climb as we came up it, and refused to take any assistance from the team car to get him through it – no food, no gel, not even an apple. I remember looking back at his face, dehydrated as anything, covered in salt, eyes dead, in his own world of deep suffering, but strangely content in it too. It was almost as if he was punishing himself for quitting earlier in the week. It was very Kiry, very Belarusian.

We're nearly back now, anyway. Enjoy these lava fields and how different they are to anything you pedal through back home. At times it's almost as if the road has been carved from the black rock like a corridor, so high and far does the lava stretch. At the top of the climb it's a mere 3km to the T-junction, then a left and a false flat for a few kilometres, kind of down, kind of up, depending on how much strength you have left in the legs. Then there's the final tiny micro-kick – 2km or so, nothing after the climbs you've done today.

Now the satisfaction can kick in, the delayed as well as the instant pleasure. If you like the sound of all this but don't fancy the big loop to the north-west, that's all good too. Just go down Bumpy to Santiago and then El Tanque, missing out Masca, or go down to Bona and then back through Masca. An out-and-back is usually less fun, but it's another way of seeing other things.

A couple more thoughts, before we leave. Remember Kiry and always take a good rain jacket and enough food. Don't look at the weather at the bottom and assume it'll be the same at the top. Don't look at the weather at the top and assume it'll be similar as you head down to the coast. Be prepared. Take full water bottles; expect bad coffee. You'll probably be just off the plane anyway, unaccustomed to the sort of heat you get on an island off the coast of north Africa, so satisfy yourself with cold beverages as often as hot. Even if you have half a bottle left, take every opportunity to refill it when you can.

Enjoy your good times on Tenerife. I had my thirtieth birthday here. We celebrated it with an ascent of Bumpy and cake at the coffee stop at the bottom. It was specially prepared by our chef. Trouble was, we were close to the Tour and that time in summer is not synonymous with fat or sugar. I'll be honest: it wasn't the greatest birthday cake I've ever had. Especially with Bumpy still to climb, we would have burned a proper slice off in moments. Sometimes, if you're going to do something for pleasure, you just have to do it properly.

# Fresh Frontiers

# La La Land

It took me a while to find Los Angeles. There's a set way of doing things in pro bike racing, an attitude that encourages you not to change gears when they're taking you places. So it was that the start of December was usually a training camp in Mallorca. January? Another camp in Mallorca or my preferred option of the Tour Down Under in Australia.

Now there's nothing wrong with those scenarios. Adelaide has given me great days of racing, plus an excellent ride for earlier in this book. Mallorca was a constant presence in my life for so long, the dependable friend who never lets you down, the smiling face you're always happy to see again. But sometimes you know when you need to see something else, when you're ready to try those fresh roads. We're escape artists, when we ride our bikes. For all the demands for calibrated climbs and well-known routes, the thrill of the not-known is stronger still.

So let's go. Hollywood, fast cars, Rodeo Drive, Beverley

Hills: we're not going to bother with any of that. Instead we're going for a ride along roads you might otherwise never find. A nod here to my team-mate Cam Wurf for his reccies in these parts and also to my fellow Cardiff boy Michael Moritz, who co-wrote Sir Alex Ferguson's last book, now lives in California and told me about friends of his who raved about the riding round here. There are climbs ahead of us, for LA can be much more up and down than you might imagine, but none of them are too long. There is sunshine, most of the time, and there are surprisingly liberated attitudes to bike riding and bike riders, when you might assume the car is still king. It is, but LA is more benevolent to its lesser wheeled subjects than you might imagine. There will be long stretches when we barely see anything with an engine, and points where we will be alone, looking down from on high over the vastness of the city and wondering how many of its residents ever come adventuring where we are now.

We'll begin in Santa Monica or Pacific Palisades. There is a more European feel to this part of the city, with roads that wiggle and waggle rather than just forming strict grids, and an actual town centre with pedestrianised streets, not just blocks of chain stores along main roads. Here you'll find good restaurants and coffee shops, an air of calm and a little bit of cool, and a fantastic beach just across from all of it.

We're straight onto the Pacific Coast Highway. I know, it sounds intimidating as well as evocative, but we'll be fine. It's wide at this point. There's a big hard shoulder and not much traffic heading out of town in the morning, plus there are plenty of other riders, for this is the route most cyclists take on their way to anywhere round here.

We head north, to Malibu. Enjoy the size and flash of the houses you pass along the way, as well as the slight pang of jealousy when you realise this world will never be yours. Unless, of course, you have a bike and legs to pedal past any time you like, in which case drink it all in. The world can be ours to share when we explore on two wheels. I had Dr Dre's house pointed out to me on one ride down this way. I imagined it would be hidden behind huge gates, some massive garden beyond, but it was right on the coast and you could see straight in. There was no conceivable way you could forget about Dre.

It's a different kind of place, Malibu, spread out over miles with no obvious centre but plenty of sights. The upmarket Malibu Nobu restaurant spills over into the Soho House private club, with its massive wraparound terrace and open-air rooms and views out over the ocean. Soho House is members-only wherever you go in the world, but the one in Malibu requires its own specific membership. Unless, that is, you do a little talk there one evening and then lead a ride for some of them, in which case you might find yourself being given a free membership for a couple of years. I've seldom felt like such a baller.

We go on through Malibu, and a cheeky bonus climb for those who fancy working the legs a little more and earning some super-nice views as payback. We turn right up Corral Canyon Road and, while we won't be short of hills today, this one is a beauty – steep, then real steep, then twisty, and all of it with sea and mountains and blue sky to lose yourself in.

It can be windy up there. I once rode it with Cam into a block headwind and it was so punchy we were either dodging flying trash cans or simply trying to keep our bikes on the road. Just take your time, because it's a long one, a good half an hour riding at tempo. A couple of times you'll think you're at the top. The houses will become more sporadic, the road even less travelled, and that's about the spot when you realise you're actually only halfway. When you do reach the end of the tarmac there's a gravel road you could keep going on, and the gravel rides round LA are awesome, but maybe that's for another book and another day.

For now, flip a U-turn and enjoy the plunging descent

back down. For some weird reason Corral Canyon is one of those roads that seems steeper on the way down than the way up, which is usually a good thing, but can catch you out if you're still staring off dreamy-eyed into the ocean views. It can get rapid, fast. Check your brakes, stay relaxed on them and stay in shape for the rest of the ride.

We're back on PCH, as us adopted locals like to call it, but only for another kilometre or two. Then it's back up climbing, this time turning right onto Latigo Canyon Drive, opposite Latigo beach. Clearly it's way too early to stop for sustenance at this point, but log the location for another time – just a little further on is a fish and chip shop which may just blow your mind. Eat on the beach as the sun is going down. Beautiful. Just get our ride done first.

Latigo is a lot shallower than Corral Canyon. It's still long and it's still twisty. There's a chef out here called Michele Lisi, who runs an Italian restaurant on Santa Monica Boulevard called Nerano and who loves his road racing, and he was the first to take me up it. I can see why it's his favourite of all the climbs around LA. The gradient jumps around, but in a good way – kicking up only to flatten out and let you recover, a lovely smooth surface, nice and wide. There's not a great deal of shade, but that's LA for you. In January it's fine. In summer expect to sweat. There are descents ahead on which you can cool.

I've done a few efforts up Latigo in my time. If there's a headwind, chill out and sit on someone's wheel instead, unless it's mine and we're friends. While I'm always happy to say hello and have a quick chat, there's nothing worse than having someone sat behind you not saying anything. Either way, it's another decent half-hour ride to the top, where we meet Kanan Dume Road, a big road heading back down to Malibu, and turn right to get further away from the coast still.

It's another short stretch until we meet Mulholland Highway and turn right once again. It's a long old road, this one, high on a ridge with big views popping around various corners, the tarmac a dividing line between the coastal hills and the mountains beyond. It runs from the bottom of the Hollywood sign all the way down to PCH much further south-west, although unfortunately there's a short section of quite techy gravel, not ideal terrain for a road bike. Today we're not on it for too long, anyway.

Should you want it, there's a road that's closed to cars not so far along, which makes a lovely descent. It's not the best maintained street in California and you may find the odd rogue rock in your way, but it's a great side-dish all the same, a twisty piece of fun that's always a pleasure to ride. If not, stay on Mulholland and roll up and down over the lumpy landscape. There's an old-fashioned iron bridge across a tiny river and then your first option for coffee – a dark wooden café that looks like something out of a Western and is literally called Old Place. It's impressive in some ways: a big set of sun-bleached antlers above the front door, always plenty of customers. Trouble is, most of them seem to be bikers. While it's always a thrill to see twenty gleaming Harleys parked up, and all those long beards and decorated leather jackets, you never get the sense that bikers have much time for their human-powered equivalents. As a result I'm yet to stop there, my assumptions also being that the coffee will be like other biker places I have inadvertently sampled in other parts of the world at other times, namely a disgusting brown liquid that looks and tastes like dishwater.

Keep an eye out for a smaller road branching off to the right called Lake Vista Drive. It's a nice stretch, this bit, taking the north side of Malibu lake, past some more delightful waterside houses with their own jetties and boats moored up alongside. It naturally curves north to take us back onto Mulholland; we keep on to a cross-roads with the busier Las Virgenes Road coming up from Malibu beach.

Still peckish? Swerved the biker place? You've got

more options here. There's always a farmer parked up on the roadside here, selling sweet-looking strawberries and punnets of blueberries from his fields. There are trucks selling Mexican food – big tacos, burritos with all the saucy trimmings – and cold Cokes out of ice boxes. Reload here by all means. Take on some water. Get a freezing Coke down you, ride the sugar and caffeine buzz over the climbs still to come.

It's Cold Canyon Road we're after next, although it's always been baking hot when I've taken it. We head right towards Monte Nido and we'll naturally find ourselves joining up with Piuma Road as it climbs left towards Saddle Peak. This is proper LA cycling territory now. Everyone love Saddle Peak, even as plenty of people fear it too.

There are four ways up it and, if you want to know more about the toughest of them, I direct you to the Las Flores chapter of the critically acclaimed *Mountains According To G*. The one we're on today is maybe the second toughest – fairly long, but the gradient is pretty consistent and there's quite a southern Spanish feel to it, the land dry and barren, the colours all somewhere between yellow and orange and brown. There are a few turns to keep you occupied; towards the top, it really opens up, and you can see down to the ocean far away on your right and the sweeping lines of the Santa Monica mountains to your left. It's a lovely climb, all in all, and one of my absolute LA favourites.

At the top, turn left and prepare to drop – fast. This is the road you could have come up on, the last few kilometres of Las Flores. You may see a number of extremely racy sports cars, for owners like to test their machines on the way up here and then pose for photographs with them and the views beyond. You see riders aplenty too.

One time up here I met a group who asked us where we were going. Turned out they were doing all four routes up Saddle Peak in the one ride, and as a reward were meeting their partners for coffee and doughnuts at the top. They invited us along. Impressed by their guts, and quite keen on the coffee and doughnuts, we joined them at the end of their adventure and had a rather nice time of it. I even randomly met the brother of my young Ineos team-mate Magnus Sheffield, which has nothing to do with the doughnuts story, but still brings up further pleasant memories.

We're on the way home now, with a few more good times before we get there. Take a left onto Schueren Road after the summit, and then down Stunt Road back to Mulholland and through to Calabasas. There might be a few more cars around these parts, but this – finally – is the café stop you've been looking for: Pedalers Fork at 23504 Calabasas Road. It looks cool, a rustic place with great décor. The food is fantastic, particularly the fried chicken sandwich and any of the burgers, and the coffee is the antithesis of the biker beverage vibe. It's also got a bike shop next door. See what I mean?

Full of belly, content of mind, take Old Topanga Canyon Road back down towards the coast. It's the quieter option in terms of traffic and there's a nice throwback hippy feel to it too. You'll see crazy homemade signs fashioned out of twigs. You'll see men with beards and women who look like they spend a lot of time sitting in the lotus position. You'll see wind chimes, dangling from the trees and ... chiming. I don't pretend to be an expert. At the top, karmically rebalanced, we're back on the main road. Then it's a super-fast descent all the way back to Topanga Beach and PCH, and onwards to wherever you might be staying.

One more tip: if you're heading on towards Pacific Palisades or Brentwood, turn off PCH onto Sunset Boulevard. The PCH pinches off a little and you lose the hard shoulder. Sunset gets busy too, but the traffic is slower and the road has more room to manoeuvre. Or, should you be ready for more kicks of a different kind, turn right and join the bike path for Santa Monica and Venice Beach.

Don't be in a rush. It's a bike path for all-comers, from joggers and young kids to those just out for a cruisy pedal, and has slight overtones of the Promenade des Anglais in Nice, if you're familiar with that.

Enjoy the sun. Don't skid out on the patches of sand that blow off the beach and onto the path, as my former Sky team-mate Ian Boswell did once. Soak in the volleyball games going on, the acrobatic bouncing on slacklines slung between the palm trees, the yoga moves and the muscle men. Push on to Santa Monica pier with its rides and theme parks.

This is the beauty of riding in LA. Get your miles in. See new roads. Drink great coffee, eventually. And, when it's all over, sit on the beach eating ice-cream or drinking beer and people-watching until the sun goes down. It doesn't have to be complicated when you do it right.

# Granada Part One

You think you've seen it all, in road riding, when you get towards your late thirties. You've ridden the big races, you've taken on the best of your generation. You've done all you can to get close and maybe just past them. You've ticked off the great climbs and ridden in places you could never have dreamed of and quite a few you've never heard of.

You're never bored and you've never become cynical, because you're riding your bike for a living, working hard without ever really working hard, but you don't imagine there will be many more surprises. And then your team tells you about a new training camp.

It's not in Tenerife this time, where you know every stretch of tarmac and every single café. It's somewhere else, where you can sleep high and train low, where there are empty roads and a proper cycling culture and a camp that doesn't feel so off-grid, even if there is something quite nice about that, too. One negative though: the accommodation is in a hotel with an evening buffet fit for a king, just not for elite riders preparing for a season of power-to-weight calculations.

Which cruel individual decided to make the dessert table the biggest? Was it the same person who placed our team's dining table in the far corner, so that every night we'd have to walk past all the temptations? Did you see the chocolate cake and the size of the pieces it was cut into?

There are, however, two sides to every coin. When we're away we take our own chef. James produces incredible food. In that hotel dining room scenario, James makes sure the final destination of the weary rider is always better than the journey. Then we have to tell all the other hotel guests that the table of food with all the reserved signs on is for the skinny ones, not those on full board. No matter how many camps I go on, it still makes me feel slightly awkward. 'Ah, she can have one piece of the salmon, hey boys?'

So let me introduce you to Granada. It's an hour to the sea, but 700 metres up and within easy striking distance of mountains so big that they'll still be covered in snow come April. The roads curl out lazily into empty countryside and vast views, and there's barely a car to bother you as you pedal out along them.

There are two routes I'm going to let you in on round here: an easy one and a tougher one. Let's say you're there for a long weekend. This is your warm-up day. Tomorrow you go long. You should use Granada itself as your base. We stay up in the Sierra Nevada and descend down, so our bodies can get the benefits of sleeping at altitude and becoming more efficient at processing oxygen, but unless you're into hiking and solitude, the city is where the fun is.

You'll know about the Alhambra. You'll recognise it even if you don't think you will. High up on a hill, looking down at everything else, it's Spanish but also so north African and Arabic. And it sets the tone for a lovely little city: different areas and districts with their own distinct feel, like Sacromonte and Albayzin, a super-nice centre with a real buzz, cheeky back-street cafés and unflashily good restaurants, as well as little boutiques if you fancy a purchase or two.

There are only two issues for us: we're not allowed to eat in the restaurants, and our legs are too tired for us to ever spend an afternoon strolling round window-shopping. And so we ride. Granada is twinned with Aix-en-Provence and I get that, having ridden around that part of southern France so much, but the countryside we pedal through reminds me more of Tuscany – olive trees flashing past as you ride, narrow roads, a rough surface under your spinning wheels.

The descents are sharp and the climbs steep. If you can, stick a granny gear to your rear cassette – maybe a 30-tooth cog to get you up without blowing your legs for whatever else is in store. It's going to be exposed, out on these roads, because the olive trees don't offer much in the way of shade, so this is a ride for late winter or early spring rather than peak summer. When we're there in April, staying way up high, there will still be people in our hotel who are heading higher still to ski, even as we're descending into the warm air down below.

Sometimes these camps can be hard – not just for what you're pushing your body through, but for what you're missing. Once you have a family of your own, watching other families enjoying holiday fun together is the surest way to bring on a sudden jolt of homesickness. If you're on holiday in Tenerife you stay down on the beaches along the coast, not on top of a dormant volcano high in the clouds, so at least in our hotel on top of Mount Teide we're on our own. We can live like monks up there, seeing only other skinny cyclists, never people eating ice-creams with their kids. So you try to look at it another way when you're in southern Spain. I'm here to work. There will be time at the other end of the year to drink beer and share big meals, to see other people and get a slice of normal life.

Speaking of other people, staying opposite my room on our last camp in Granada was ex-Swansea City player and manager, Garry Monk. My coach Conor got chatting to him one day in the hotel lobby.

'Hey, do I know you from somewhere?'

'I don't know ... maybe?'

'Didn't I play football or cricket with you? Where are you from?'

'Bedford.'

'Hmm, I guess not, but I'm sure I know you.'

'Maybe from me playing football at Swansea?'

'Ah shit – Garry Monk!'

To the good stuff. This route begins on the sort of lovely twisty roads that always keep you interested. There's always a bend to lean round, another corner ahead to get out of the saddle and work towards. There's a special couple of kilometres early on that take you along the side of a mountain in a flat horseshoe, a huge great view stretching away to your left across the hills. At this point, still close in to the fringes of the city, there are always runners and hikers about, dogs being walked, little kids on bikes too big for them. It's got the feel of the roads out of Los Angeles around the famous Hollywood sign: red soil, big blue skies, a warmth that means you're fine in a short-sleeved jersey and shorts.

It's the gravel sections next, as you work your way through the area around the town of Beas de Granada. The road sweeps sharply left and right, and it can feel like you're going to get lost in all those olive trees, but it's the sounds I always notice here – the crunch under your tyres, the beep of your Garmin telling you where to go and what lies ahead.

We all know gravel is hip these days. Enjoy it for that reason. You can imagine, too, you're in an Iberian version of Strade Bianche, the roads not quite as white as in Tuscany and the vegetation not quite as lush, but the same sensation of the bike underneath you and the wild, ancient feel to it all. When you have ridden down from the Sierra Nevada, the air feels thicker – not the sharp intake of air you get at altitude, but a mugginess, an intensity. It's comforting on your skin after the fresh descent, but you feel it, too, as you begin to pick up the pace.

You'll have to work hard, but you never need to go too deep. That's the beauty of this ride. Tenerife is either up or down. Around Granada, you can cruise. If you're aiming to tick off all the rides in this book, I'd do the UK ones first, building your fitness, then come here. Granada will help you. Granada is your friend. Only hit Tenerife when you're sure you're at your best.

In some of the tiny little villages you pass through now it's as if you've travelled back in time thirty years, as well as an hour from the big city. There are few signs of life. Those that you do see are life being lived in comfortable slow motion. An old lady wobbling her way from her house to see the neighbours, an old boy getting his daily bread from the bakery off the main square. You see other old boys sat out in deckchairs watching the world go by, and you feel slightly guilty that you're clattering through at such a speed, because they'll only get ten seconds of stimulation from you before waiting another hour for the next thing to happen.

They're all one-way roads, these ones through the villages. Depending on what time of day you set off, you might not see a car for hours. At rush hour there could be the odd one parked up outside an ancient garage or mechanics shop, but at siesta time these places can be like ghost towns – which perversely makes it all the more important that you prime yourself for a car arriving from nowhere at every junction, because they're not expecting to see anyone either, so are unlikely to have bothered braking in advance or considered indicating.

There's driving with due caution and there's coming in hot like the pensioners of southern Spain do – straight through junctions, turning left across you without warning.

You can't get too angry about it, because it's their manor, but do keep your eyes peeled. And if the rickety cars don't get you, the dogs hopefully won't either. I'm never sure if they're actually strays or there is just no need to put them on a lead because there's nowhere for them to run away to.

You don't tend to be the biggest fan of dogs, as a bike rider. They like to chase you too much and, if they can't get a decent mouthful of your calf, look like they'd like to bite your tyres. However, the dogs in this part of the world seem quite placid, happy to wander around sniffing things. Pure and simple dog good times. If you don't bother them, they shouldn't bother you.

You can stay off the main roads round here. There's usually a decent hard shoulder, so you're not right up against the fast traffic, but it can get quite windy with the big trucks coming past. No-one likes that sensation of being sucked along and out in a juggernaut's slipstream. You'll often find a bike path tucked behind some barriers and, while they can sometimes be full of rubbish lobbed out of those speeding cars, they're also a lot safer. It's harder for us to use them when we're cycling in a group, two riders abreast at the front, but if you're solo or just cruising with a couple of mates on your wheel then they can be your friend. When I rode up from the airport to our hotel in the mountains I used bike paths almost all the way, and they were lovely.

We're on a loop today, which is always the best sort of ride. The worst? A straight out-and-back, because you can't help thinking that with every pedal stroke you're making things more difficult for yourself on the way back in. It's dry and dusty coming back into Granada, only the odd runner plodding down a dirt path, and it reminds me a little of the desert scenery you see in *Breaking Bad* – the colour of the soil, the wire fences falling down or leaning in the wind. You can't even work out what the fences are supposed to be demarcating, because there's no livestock about, just the sun and a group of skinny men keen to get home and pile into some food.

Finishing Liège-Bastogne-Liège can feel the same. It's a fantastic race, one of cycling's Monuments, and I love riding it, but the last 10km is not the best. They bring you through the arse-end of Liège and that's sort of what I'm doing now in Granada. It'll all be worth it shortly, I promise.

Maybe you've still got some power in the legs and adventure in your heart. If so, there's a couple of punchy dead-end climbs you can throw in as bonus sections before you call it a day, both of them finishes at the Vuelta in recent years.

The first takes you from La Zubia, just south of the city, to Cumbres Verdes. It's where Alejandro Valverde beat Chris Froome on stage six of the 2014 race, the year Alberto Contador won the GC and Froomey came second. Last time I was there we did some activation and some lactate testing – nothing flat out, but a good little test. As I was working hard, a guy in a jeep drove past and stopped to chat. Turned out he was British and lived up there, although I still had a job to do and couldn't really give him my full conversational charm. You can't, when a climb is like this – dead straight, an average of 10.5%, about 3.8km. It took me just under fifteen minutes that day, pushing an average of 350 watts. Like I say, an activation session, not a race day.

The other one is the climb up to Sierra de la Alfaguara, which looks more normal and has more switchbacks, and is 12.4km at an average of 5.4%. It was the finish on stage four in 2018, the year Simon Yates won the race. When I rode it there were a few kids rock-climbing on the cliffs, shouting encouragement at us as we went past. They got a bidon from me by way of thanks.

Actually, there's one more, but I'm just a bit embarrassed to tell you about it. It's the little road up to Pinos Genil, which obviously we rebranded as Penis. I know. The climb starts slow, gets steeper and then becomes twisty in the trees. You can smell meat cooking on open-air barbecues, and see locals sitting out with their cervezas and big bowls of chips. It's a particular kind of cruel torture to us and can send us all a bit mad, because it is exactly what you want in summer, but it's never a bad idea to get a bit of climbing in the legs, especially as our second route in Granada is a fair amount harder than this one.

In the meantime, the rest of us are on our way back into Granada through the industrial area. It's less Alhambra here and more last impromptu restroom for the weary cyclist. You'd think no-one would mind you stopping for a pee when you're doing so on a pile of rubbish that includes a few dirty nappies and a dead rat, but the beeps from the car that passed us on that occasion would suggest not.

It's only a brief section though, this part, and you're travelling at pace, so you're soon back in the sweet heart of the city. And as you ride in, cruising now, it's always good to see ordinary life going on when you've been stuck at the top of a mountain.

In terms of coffee places for your post-ride pleasure, there's Noat Coffee on Plaza de los Girones, which is a nice little stop. It's quiet, but you can sit outside. The only slight hitch is that there's only a big enough patch of sunlight coming through the buildings for two of you to sit in the sun, unless you want to rotate every fifteen minutes. We ended up there most days on our training camp and spent so much we half-expected a free coffee at some stage.

About 200m down the same cobbled street is a really nice bakery. I was on the full diet regime at that time of year, a world of steamed fish and salad, but the cookies in there were the best I've ever had – crunchy on the outside, nice and gooey in the middle. As for the brownies, there's a blondie, a Kinder one ... Go there as a non-elite rider and make up for all the eating we weren't allowed to do.

One more for you: Malamiga on Calle San Anton does really good coffee, plus there are benches outside where you're in the sun all day. If you're in a big group there's a little less space, but the brownies are still exceptional. Ask them to bag some up, take them back to your family for tea and in the process win the literal brownie points to get you out for your longer ride before you fly home. Perfect.

# The Adrenaline Capital of the World

I'd always wanted to go to New Zealand. There's an affinity with the place, if you come from Wales: the love of rugby, the landscape. Okay, the sheep, but let that be the last mention of them. At the start of 2023 it all finally came together. I was racing at the Tour Down Under in Adelaide in January, and I had Sa and Macs with me. I was due to go training in California afterwards, but I had a gap in between. Why not, I thought, fly three hours across the Tasman, take my bike with me, hire a campervan and do it properly as a family?

When I say do it properly, what I mean of course, is do it properly as a professional road cyclist. Which meant Sa doing the driving and most of the childcare, and me heading out on my bike for hours every day, albeit with some excellent breakfasts and coffee stops with wife and son in a number of spectacularly scenic locations.

Because it turns out New Zealand is a sensational place to visit, and a similarly fantastic place to ride your bike. There aren't heaps of different roads, but that's fine, because all of them take you through the sorts of places you love to go on your bike – river valleys, coastal roads, high mountain passes – and with almost no traffic anywhere you pedal. I admitted it to myself pretty early on: okay, New Zealand – you're like a bigger, better Wales.

Our trip was planned to precision, maybe on an 80/20 split between Sa and me. Well, precision once we realised hiring a campervan for ten days meant hiring it for a minimum of a month and that leaving it to the last minute made it like renting a mansion. So hotels and Airbnbs it was, with Sa doing the research, planning the stops (seven in total) and booking everything. I brought to the table a rough idea of what I could ride in between, and planned the routes. Fair enough, a 90/10 split.

Back to New Zealand vs. Wales. North Island has the rolling countryside, like you find in the Vale in south Wales. That was leg five, around Rotorua. It has other parts like a supersized Brecon Beacons. This was in the South Island, on the first leg from Christchurch to Lake Tekapo. It's not just the trees and big open spaces. It came with drizzle and enough wind to get annoying, but it also has mountains that, to be totally honest, make Snowdonia look almost quaint.

We spent an extra day or so at the end in Auckland, thanks to bad weather and flooding. Again, just like Wales. The big city was the first time in nine days we'd experienced a traffic jam. Until that moment the stickiest patch of the entire trip had been five cars long. I rode past lake after lake in North Island, even if storms meant we couldn't explore the wild stretches of the Coromandel Peninsula as we had hoped. But the best riding I found? Around Queenstown, in South Island.

There's always something refreshing about riding new roads. The stimulation for your head seems to stimulate the legs too. The variation in the landscape of South Island and the heavy, sticky roads mean you can very rarely cruise for long. And since I was mixing up my training anyway, switching from the usual long and slow/low carb regime (*so* 20-teens in the elite world) to going shorter but quicker, nothing crazy but always pushing, I was a long way from ever being bored. In January, too, the weather is great: lots of sun, never too hot, never much need for more than a short-sleeved jersey with a gilet or light jacket for the chill on some of the more sustained descents.

So we start our loop in Queenstown itself, not least because that's probably where you'll end up staying. It's certainly where you'll be going out. There's so much going on, so much to do. It's got the coffee shops. It's got the bars. It's got every conceivable adventure sport, from the classics – hello, bridge bungee – to the ones that are way too intense for me (no thanks, sky-diving). You can paraglide, you can parascend or you can bottle it and go for a speedboat ride with your three-year-old son instead, although in my defence the jetboat performed a range of impressive spins and accelerations and sprayed its passengers with cold water on a number of occasions. Macs loved it. You can decide for yourself whether he was holding my hand or if I was holding his.

We'll begin with an optional climb, should you be feeling strong, or fancy a warm-up challenge the day before your big ride. Our destination is the Coronet Peak ski station, and we'll take Gorge Road north out of town and then Arthurs Point Road. It's all signposted, so that bit is straightforward. But there's nothing easy about the climb itself, although you can always spin in a smaller gear and enjoy the views, which will take your breath away if the gradient somehow doesn't. It's just under 8.5km from bottom to top, with an average gradient of 9%. That's about thirty minutes of riding for me in

January shape and form, pedalling by myself rather than racing myself into pieces.

You gain more than 700m of altitude, which is a lot to start the day, so make sure you've hit at least one of those excellent coffee shops in town before setting off. In my two days in Queenstown I enjoyed this climb so much I did it five times, and each time I got the same vibes: distinctively Pyrenean, quite twisty, steep enough at the bottom to put off the dabblers and the faint-hearted. It's a heavy old road under your tyres, which is fine, because you're doing this for the experience rather than the time, and the trees all around help keep you cool if the sun is coming in a little punchy. Off to your right-hand side it's all open views. Remember, this book is about the pleasures of a great ride as much as the pain, so take the time to look around and breathe it all in and celebrate being out on your bike in a beautiful place with nothing to do but pedal on.

Around halfway up is Skippers Road, which according to a link I clicked on in Google at the start of that day deserves a place in the top ten most dangerous roads in the world. Of course, I was tempted to experience its thrills for myself – I'm the sort of man who does jet-boat rides suitable for three-year-olds – but sadly my training schedule was against me. You know how it is.

I say the average gradient is 9%. The key word in that sentence is average. This is not a steady regular road. It has ramps well above 10% and flatter sections where you can try to recover a little, but it all adds to the stimulation. The hairpins give you a target to chase around; the top of the peak is almost always visible and so seems within reach, even when you've actually got at least another ten minutes of effort to come. There are hardly any cars going up there in summer and plenty of mountain-bikers coming chasing down the network of trails through the forest, so this is a place for you and your bike to feel together and a team.

The descent is just as much fun. You can flow round most of it, although a couple of the corners tighten up on the exit, so keep your wits about you. And then we're on with the main ride, or picking up those of you who didn't fancy the Coronet hors d'oeuvre, which is absolutely fine.

We'll head on along Malaghans Road to Arrowtown, which gives you the opportunity to grab another coffee if you've done the climb, or to fill your jersey pockets with cakes for the road ahead. (My personal favourite is a café called Provisions, with its quality flat white and brownies capable of fuelling you for a good number of riding hours.) We'll eventually drop down along McDonnell Road to Highway 6 and Arrow Junction. If you're coming straight from Queenstown, you can also follow 6 through Frankton and along the shore of the lake to pick up the rest of the ride here.

Pick a good day and you'll meet plenty of fellow travellers. On one of my rides I bumped into the young FDJ rider Reuben Thompson, who I'd ridden the Tour Down Under with a couple of weeks before. Being pro riders, the first thing we discussed was the best coffee shops. This being New Zealand, the conversation went on for some time and reflected upon the happy fact that Kiwi cafés frequently not only roast their own beans on site, but manage not to be totally up themselves about it at the same time.

At Arrow Junction, turn left off 6 onto the Crown Range Road towards Wānaka. This is one of the easier sets of directions you'll find in this book. The road goes over the Crown Range mountains and ends up in Wānaka, so if you go wrong at this point I'm taking no responsibility for it.

This is our busiest section of the route. It's also the country's highest tarmacked road, so keep an eye out for campervan drivers both enjoying the scenery and occasionally looking at it too much, rather than the twists and turns ahead of them. You may occasionally get tourists enjoying it all so much they forget which side of the road they're meant to be on – and if you think any of these criticisms are aimed at Sa, you would of course be wrong. Anyway, the road is wide enough for everyone. There's nothing to stress about and everything to enjoy.

It's steep, this first section. It's switchbacks and deep breaths, with a potential sense of unease about what lies ahead, so it's worth calibrating your brain for what you're about to do; Queenstown to Wānaka all the way is almost 70km. There and back in one day is quite the undertaking. You can see why you might leave Coronet Peak for another day, so by all means aim for the Crown Range summit look-out point, which is 30km from Queenstown, take some photos and enjoy the descent back into the (comparative) big smoke. You'll still have a couple of good hours of riding in your legs, you'll have had the views and the coffee, and you'll still have the appetite to enjoy the evening's escapades.

There's many things I love about riding my bike: the distances you can travel, the speeds you can go, the places it can take you. And I love the fact that you're out and about in the real world, meeting people, talking to them, sharing your experiences. When I got to the summit of this road one time, I came across another random rider pedalling in shorts, flip-flops and no top. He was riding the length of New Zealand, entirely on his own, with just two panniers' worth of clothes, camping gear and supplies with him. If you play football for a living, you don't end up having a kickabout with a stranger in the street. Pro golfers don't tee off alongside punters struggling to go round in less than 100 shots. Cycling? Same roads, same climbs and descents, same round wheels. You never know who you're going to bump into.

The summit is 1,121m up. That's a lot of views when the air is as clean as it is in New Zealand. If you're lucky, you can see the brown hills and the green valleys and the snow on top of the distant peaks. You can see big old birds circling overhead, and old trees twisted and blown sideways by the winter winds. You can also see plenty of sheep, although we agreed we weren't going to talk about them again, so let's get on with the descent down towards Wānaka.

It's a good steep plunge, the first 5km. You can enjoy it, because the road surface is good and the bends wide enough to get those big old campervans round, so a skinny racing bike has no issues at all. For the next 25km it gradually turns into one of those lovely false flats where you can't quite discern the gradient and instead think you must just be on a great day or significantly fitter than you had previously given yourself credit for. Only when you turn around and come back the other way will you get a true appreciation of how this road really is, but for now enjoy the rolling pasture and farmers' fields and distant sheep – done it again – and think about the drink and snack, or rather drinks and lunch, you're going to enjoy when you reach the lakefront in Wānaka itself.

On your way through the Cardrona Valley, keep an eye out for a wire fence with what I would guess is close to 1,000 bras hanging on it. That's no exaggeration. Apparently the local authorities keep trying to take them all down and local others – plus tourists – keep replacing them with fresh ones. Now that is something you don't get in Merthyr Tydfil.

There are those in these parts who will tell you they prefer Wānaka to Queenstown. Same sort of spectacular location (lakes, river, mountains), half as many people. Still great coffee and cafés, and proper farmer-sized portions for the hungry amongst us, but a sense of chill you don't always get when people are lobbing themselves off bridges on elastic or launching themselves out of planes.

Being the sociable sort I am, plus the rugby obsessive, I got in contact with former All Blacks captain Richie McCaw when I was there and went out for a ride with him. I knew Richie had got into his cycling since retiring after winning those two Rugby World Cups. I'd also heard that when he gets into something he really goes for it. He flies gliders out of a little town called Omarama about seventy minutes' drive north-east along Highway 8, and he's a helicopter pilot too. I just didn't expect him to be quite as useful on a bike as he turned out to be, and not only because I've gone on rides with Wales superstar winger George North and it's like taking a fifty-year-old man with you. A very heavy fifty-year-old man.

We were out for a couple of hours. I hadn't bothered with any breakfast, expecting a gentle spin of the pedals, a chat about how fortunate New Zealand were to beat Wales at the 2003 World Cup, and something about the flukes and strokes of bad luck that have prevented Wales from beating the All Blacks since before Elvis had his first number one.

Instead, we were banging out an average of 300 watts for the entire time. On the short climbs he would use his old open-side flanker power to launch up to 600 watts. On the longer climbs he got his head down and ground it out. I expected a coffee early on and then a wave as I departed for Queenstown, but Richie is not a man for stopping – not for coffee after 20km or, in fact, at junctions or roundabouts. He doesn't have to. New Zealand stops when Richie McCaw comes into town. The cars wait. They do the waving. I did the no-breakfast regret.

So take on the food you need when you're in Wānaka. Maybe wheel your bike on to the pebbly beach, take your shoes and socks off and dip your toes in the cool water. And as you're pedalling back home, reflecting on how much fun you've had, try to figure out if you have the time and legs before you move on to take in one more Queenstown riding treat.

It's called the Remarkables. It's a ski station in winter, and it's a beaut of a road for us lot when the sun is shining and the weather is sweet. It's easy to find from Queenstown – Highway 6 through Frankton and then Kawarau Falls, turning left when you see the signpost. A climb even quieter than Coronet Peak and a road most of us would agree is tougher still, it's just over 13km from bottom to top, an average gradient of 10%, an elevation gain of almost 1300m, the last bit on gravel. Don't be put off by the closed gate at the bottom. That's just to keep cars at bay. It simply means you'll have the road all to yourself – the hairpins, the relentless steepness, the views down to the little airport and across the lake to Kingston.

Usually there's a sense of sadness when you fly out of a place where you've had so much fun, and there was a little of that when we left Queenstown to head up to North Island. But as I climbed Coronet Peak on my final morning, a guy in a car came up alongside me and beeped. He pulled over, we had a photo and a chat, and it turned out he worked with someone who went to the same school in Cardiff, Whitchurch High, as me (and Sam Warburton and Gareth Bale). He told me he was working in town and invited me over. I would have popped in, but I was so keen on the riding round there that I'd almost run out of time. I was riding straight to the airport from the descent, meeting Sa and Macs there, and having a Belgian shower in the car park before running for our flight. And if you don't know what a Belgian shower is, I'll say only two things: it doesn't take long, and you don't smell great.

# Granada Part Two

Okay. So we've had one great day in the Sierra Nevada around Granada. Now it's time for the big one. Harder, longer, steeper. Which we all know, because we're all riders here, means more fun.

It's a climb, as we leave Granada behind us to the north-west. We're heading for the village of Monachil on the GR-3202 and a piece of road known locally as the Alto del Purche. For an hors d'oeuvre to the main feast, it's quite substantial – just over 9km long with an average gradient of 7.6% – and the sort of steep start to clear any remaining cobwebs, followed by an eye-watering finale.

At least you know what's coming. When I arrived in Granada for the first time I had the smart idea of getting some cheeky extra training in by riding from the airport, which is to the west of the city, all the way to the team hotel high in the Sierra Nevada. The team told me not to worry bringing wheels for my road bike, as they would bring some down from the hotel. Unfortunately that message had got mixed up somewhere between the emails and the mechanic meeting me at the arrivals terminal of Aeropuerto Federico García Lorca Granada-Jaén. There were no wheels, just my time-trial bike looking all sleek and shiny on top of the car.

Now time-trial bikes are a joy to ride when you're time-trialling, when you want a nice big gear to push and a slippery aero tuck to hold, but when you start following a route pre-programmed into the Garmin attached to the stem of your handlebars and the road starts kicking up at close to 10%, you appreciate their specific set-up slightly less.

There wasn't much wind as I ground my way up. There's no small 39 x 30 gearing on my TT machine, and neither is there a great deal of shade or shelter on this road. Monachil is a climb to be enjoyed in spring or autumn and endured in high summer. However, it's a proper one – that's what you want when you're training for a Grand Tour, as I was, or subconsciously seeking stories to tell your friends back home, as you may well be.

It did amuse the rest of the team when I eventually reached our hotel and sat down for dinner a damp and weary mess.

'How was the drive?'

'I rode it. On my TT bike.'

'So you didn't come up Monachil, then?'

'No idea, but it was a right bastard. Through a little town and kicks straight up.'

'The little town of Monachil?'

'Okay. Please stop laughing now.'

We did it again a few days later, this time as a conservative team effort, me with the sort of gears you want when the first 6km average 9.5%. I maintained around 350 watts. If you have a power meter of your own and you'd care for a comparison, it took us twenty-eight minutes from the very bottom to the top. Those first 6km will feel steep. Then it's all a little uneven, and even drops down for maybe 900m with a couple of kilometres to go before climbing back up to the top, but it will get a good sweat going for this first part of the day. It will also transition you thoroughly and effectively from lounging at the hotel to the sort of adventure you'll remember as long as you're riding. It's twisty, it's got big views and you'll meet lots of other bike riders. Some will overtake you, others will be overtaken – which is the most straightforward definition of racing there is.

At the top you could turn right onto the A-395 for the main road up to Sierra Nevada, but we'll go downhill for a couple of kilometres towards the village of Pinos Genil. You'll recall from the previous chapter our nickname for it; I'll say nothing more on the subject. It's a safe descent, a wide road with a smooth surface quite used to the temperature extremes that'll hit it over the course of its four seasons, so go as fast as you want to. When you get close to Penis – I beg your pardon, Pinos Genil – the descent gets even better. It's a smaller road, but it still has two lanes, it still has nice tarmac and it's still pleasingly twisty. It's the sort of downhill to build your confidence if your home territory is a little flatter or you're still getting used to the speed good road bikes can go when you encourage them to do so.

Into the town with two names. Turn right, on to the GR-3200 and prepare for a draggy section, which isn't really a climb but certainly isn't flat either. The road surface now is grippy and the legs are whinging a little, reminding you they've already taken care of more than thirty minutes of climbing, but also appreciating the chance to warm up again after the free ride of the descent.

There's some good stuff for your eyes and general mood as you head on towards the next town of Güéjar Sierra. There are restaurants in Italy that appear underwhelming from the outside, the building pretty average and the signage almost apologetic. Then you realise how many people are going in to eat there, so you join them and you understand that the exterior doesn't matter when the food they're knocking out is so outstanding. That's how it feels in Güéjar Sierra, too, as you ride past places and see how much fun the punters are having and how good their plates look and how tempting their glasses. You can sense the relaxation and you can feel much of the same vibe you find in Granada's own backstreets – the cobbles, the unobtrusive wealth, the outdoor living. And because it's Spain, you'll always get the same old boys and old girls sitting outside their houses or on benches in the shade of big trees around the square, watching the world go by and wondering when bicycles became so fast.

You see domesticated animals wandering about as you leave the town and get out on to the rocky hillsides; the same contented-looking cows, the same goats with great curly horns like the regimental ones that do a lap of the pitch at the Principality Stadium before Wales games. A few of the boys look at those horns and the inscrutable faces underneath them and get nervous about a rogue charge. Much as this would be amusing to see – considerably more amusing than a team-mate riding a brutal climb on a TT bike, for example – it has yet to come to pass. The goats retreat into the rocks and we pedal onwards towards the centrepiece of our big day out.

You appreciate all you see, as a rider: the stimulation

of the scenery, the challenge of the road. I have ridden the Tour de France twelve times, I've done the Dauphiné loads; I've raced to the sun with Paris-Nice. France feels like a second home. I love Italy and all the charming quirkiness it brings, but until 2023 I had ridden the Vuelta a España just once, only really racing in Spain at the Volta a Catalunya, where the roads and the culture are very different to where we are today. So in my seventeen years in the pro ranks, until recently I had barely experienced this sort of landscape: drier and more barren, the roads more cracked and grippy, the climbs more inconsistent, shallow and then steep.

All this is a good thing. Familiarity is a comfort but it also deadens your senses. I know we all like ordering the same dish when we go out for a curry, but sometimes the takeaway you'll remember for longest will be the one plucked from a menu sub-section you've never visited before, even if the after-effects of the spice levels do blow your doors off the next morning.

By the way, if you hadn't noticed, we're on a short, steep descent. We fizz across a narrow bridge, wiggle left and then take a ninety-degree right and begin to climb, with almost no speed to carry with us, on the A-4030.

Take courage at this point, because you're about to be tested. This was the route taken by stage fifteen of the

Vuelta in 2022, when my young Ineos team-mate Thymen Arensman won the stage on his way to sixth in the GC and Remco Evenepoel took a firm grip on overall. From Güéjar all the way to the finish line that day (and we can go further, should we choose) was just short of 20km at an average gradient of almost 8%, so you'll see we're not playing games.

The ski resort at the top, in Sierra Nevada itself, sits between 2000m and 2300m, with the finish line of this stage at 2500m. And getting there is harder than Monachil, because it's more sustained. The corners are super-steep up the inside, so the temptation is to level them off a fraction by going round the outside, but there will be riders and a few cars coming down the other way, so be careful. I say cars; I saw maybe two or three in the three times I did this climb, but you never know, and you may be riding at a busier time of year. What you won't see is many people. There is only the occasional house. You ride past them and wonder what it would be like to live there. Mainly I wonder what swear words you'd come out with when you made the long slog back home from the distant supermarket and remembered you'd forgotten the milk.

The big win, for all of us, thanks to the Vuelta coming this way so recently? The excellent resurfacing job they did with the tarmac. It means that when you're doing a big team effort, ramping up through the heart-rate zones across twenty minutes and going pretty much full gas for the last five of them, you're getting full value for what you're putting through the pedals. It's a good climb for teams rehearsing for the big days in the high mountains at the great races, not least because everyone has to work as hard as everyone else. You can be sitting second wheel and still have to put out the same power as the rider in front, because there is no aero drag to mention here. It's too steep for too long to go fast enough to create any.

When you get to the junction towards the top, you have a couple of options. You can turn right towards the Repsol petrol station and the main road further on, but it's more fun to go left, not least because cars aren't allowed on this stretch. If you aren't sure whether you're on the right road, you'll pass a sign saying as much. Our Ineos team car tried following us on one ride and got stopped and told off by the police. Thymen attempted to pacify them by handing over one of his bottles as a goodwill gesture. The policeman then said he needed one for his colleague in the car, so I gave him mine, which made it all the more galling when they refused to help us out and we had to crack on solo. There do seem to be more policemen in Sierra Nevada than the population or level of crime justify. My soigneur Marko went for a walk one day from our hotel, keen to get to the highest point in the mountain range at 3300m, and a policeman stopped him and sent him home. Apparently he had the wrong shoes on, as if the summit was some sort of exclusive nightclub rather than a pleasant viewing point.

Still, these are super-quiet roads up here. We're in the trees for some of it, so there's occasionally some welcome shade, and we're so high that the air is cooler. I don't pretend to entirely understand the science – why is it colder when you're closer to the sun? – but I do appreciate it when my skin feels it. We're twisting, too, which always makes a hard climb pass more easily, and there are fine views out to the left, although because you can't see the sea, you weirdly never feel as high as you do in Tenerife, even though the bottom of the climb in Granada is higher than the starting point for our great rides in Tenerife.

We're on this stretch for about 8km. At the first junction, turn left and continue climbing for a further 3km if you want to get up to 2300m, or turn right to drop back down to the main road and a short stretch into the bottom of Sierra. At 2300m there's the big sports complex on Calle del Torcal, the Centro de Alto Rendimiento de Sierra Nevada, or CAR for short. You'd think it would be the natural place for us to stay – in our time up there I've seen elite French swimmers, Ironman triathletes and middle-distance runners on the outdoor track – but they won't let our chef do his own thing in their kitchens, which is a prerequisite for us, so we stay in a normal hotel full of normal people, which suits us much better.

Imagine it. You can look out of your hotel room window and see the snow on the tops, the skiers coming back down the slopes like little black dots against the bright white. You can hear the fun and the laughter, which perversely makes the fact you've been grovelling up a series of enormous hills slightly easier to take. You look at the skiers all rugged up in their woolly hats and gloves, glance down at your own Lycra shorts and thin short-sleeved jersey and think, yeah, they might be able to smash down a few beers in the party tent, but they're clearly not quite as tough as we are.

If you so choose, and a well-deserved beverage is calling your name, you can hang that right I just mentioned, dropping down on to the A-395 and left into Sierra for an apres-ski, or turn left and head all the way back to Granada. You'll be descending back down to 700m and it's a good old long one for you to enjoy.

Or, if you're feeling fruity, you can carry on climbing a little more, past a barrier to stop cars going any further.

Make sure your bottles are full and your pockets packed with snacks, because if you run out of fuel and bonk here, it's still a long way up. The barrier is at 2500m, and if you're feeling good and you've got something warm for the descent – you could always ask one of the skiers for an emergency loan – then nip round it and see how high you can get.

We managed to get up to 2800m in the spring before the snow got too deep and we had to turn around. In summer? You could make it all the way to 3300m. According to my team-mate Ben Swift, it's the highest paved road in Europe. That fact hasn't been checked though, and because it comes from Swifty, I'm not 100% confident in it, although it does sound pretty good. Either way, just make sure you've got the right shoes on for that nightclub at the top.

# Friends and the Future

# West is Best

The world of elite road racing is changing. That's a good thing in lots of ways – young riders attacking every stage of the big three-week Grand Tours, team tactics having to respond, riders not settling for being pigeonholed as one sort of specialist but wanting instead to break down the old barriers and have fun wherever they care to point their front wheels.

At the same time, you can find yourself getting early-onset old-man grumps as you pedal through your mid-thirties towards one of the bigger landmarks in your life. You find yourself watching the great races and muttering phrases like, 'Easy, son, you've got a big day ahead tomorrow,' and 'Why's he doing that there?' as well as 'I don't recognise that kit,' and 'How can he be born in that year?'

Which is why it was such a pleasing experience to go riding in west Wales with my young compatriot Josh Tarling, when he joined Ineos for the 2023 season. Josh is eighteen years younger than me, which I find deeply upsetting. He was born in a year that seems impossibly recent to me. The fact that when I was busy winning the Tour in 2018 he was waiting for his voice to break makes me feel quite angry.

He is, however, quite the rider. British time-trial champion in 2023, bronze at the World Championship's time trial, 6' 4" tall, a boy born for the Classics if ever there was one. He also hails from Aberaeron in Ceredigion, and knows all the lanes and sharp little climbs and descents in west Wales far better than I did before I rode them with him.

So a lot of this ride is Josh's inside knowledge, even if it's my legs and your legs now too. I'm going to split it into two sections, as well: Mumbles to St Clears via Llanelli on the first day and then a slice of coastal joy from Newgale to Aberaeron the next. You could do the first as a there-and-back if you're feeling strong, but I'd advise you to treat these as a pair of point-to-points. Sure, you'll need someone to meet you at the end of each day with your kit and possibly a car, but that's just another fine example of the teamwork that lies behind all great road-riding success stories. It also means we'll never be retracing our steps, never having that slightly doomy feeling that can take hold on an out-and-back when you know every pedal stroke in one direction adds another pedal stroke to your day's ride home.

Mumbles, then, home to some of the finest Welsh rugby players of their generation, because of Ospreys' location in Swansea, and home to many a Swansea City player, because of Swansea City FC's location in Swansea. It's a lovely place, Mumbles, all headlands and beaches and the Gower peninsula just beyond. You can ride the roads of the Gower if you like and you'll find even more great beaches, but I'm going to follow the bike path along the coastal road, through the gentle washes of sand if there's a stiff breeze coming off the bay, enjoying the sun on my back when it's summer and the weather is smiling on us. You may even want to break one of our usual rules and start the day with an ice-cream from Joe's, with its blue shop front and stripey awning. There's a reason why Joe's is famous in these parts. If you don't want to take my word for it, last time I was riding through here I spotted former Wales rugby captain Ryan Jones tucking into a gelato, so there you go.

We'll cut up north-westwards before we get into the middle of Swansea itself, head through Gowerton and then past Loughor Castle and over the river towards Llanelli, riding straight past Parc y Scarlets, which oozes history. It's like going back in time, but there's no denying the calibre of rugby player to have walked into that stadium. I'm still yet to go there to watch a game. Being a Cardiff boy, the Blues or now Cardiff Rugby has always been my team, but I've always had a soft spot for Llanelli or the Scarlets thanks to my dad.

The B4303 will take us along the coast, becoming the A484 as it goes through Pembrey with its big, wide beach at low tide and on to Kidwelly and north again. Pembrey holds fond memories of racing on its closed moto racing circuit, while the Tour of Britain started there one year, which was quite the buzz. Racing in Britain is so rare that it's always a thrill, even more so in Wales. When one of my aunties found out we were starting in Pembrey, she decided to have a quiet word with my dad. 'Tell Geraint to stop at the usual pub. I'll be there with some friends. He should say hello . . .'

Back to the ride. It's quite up and down round here, the roads rolling once we get away from the coast. It's part of the backstory of the Thomas family too. My dad's side of the family are all from the St Clears area, but because he was one of the younger brothers, he was never going to inherit the family farm. Instead he was sent to seek his fortune at the coal-fired power station in Aberthaw, down on the coast near Barry, which led quite quickly to him deciding to try the bright lights of Cardiff instead. From the big smoke to the bigger smoke and with it another significant upturn for him: he met my mum.

We would still go visiting in St Clears when I was a kid. My nan was there, and she was a woman who believed in the outdoor life. Vegetables were grown fresh in her garden. My brother and I used to love going down to visit. We'd play out in the fields, down by the train tracks, in the river, the townies having a whale of a time. You'd notice, as a youngster, how the veg tasted different to back home. Mmm, good and fresh, my parents would say, nodding approvingly. The usual stuff from Tesco tastes better, I would think, not quite daft enough to say it out loud.

So these roads bring back those memories. As I pedal past I recognise the same streets and shops and fields that I used to see out of the window of the family car as we drove west. The same distinctive smells of the countryside are in the air, the clouds blowing in from the west and the coast beyond.

That's where we're starting our second route, when you've absorbed this first one. You can carry on from St Clears if you choose – get closer to the starting point of day two, dip down to Tenby and its palm trees and twin beaches, or west to the deep water ports of Pembroke and Milford Haven, to Marloes and St Brides and Little Haven. Maybe end day one with a dip in the sea to sort your legs out, for the next day brings much more up and down than you might expect when we're nowhere near the mountains and the coast is our constant companion.

We'll roll into Newgale to begin, possibly from Druidston and Nolton Haven to the south, or on the A487 if you're coming from an overnight in Haverfordwest. You descend right down to the cove, with the campsite at the bottom of Wood Hill, right along with the beautiful beach off to your left-hand side, past a couple of pubs (no, it's too early for the Duke of Edinburgh Inn) and then do the long climb back out onto the headland again. It's all rather like an inverted west Walian version of Horseshoe Pass, all those miles north, outside Ruthin in Denbighshire. Rather than riding up in a great U-shape for spectacular views, you're dropping down.

Keep the coast to your left, ride up through Penycwm and Solva, and go through St Davids. It won't take you long; it's the smallest city in the UK. At the same time, there's no point in rushing it. You couldn't, if you wanted to – its status and the beautiful cathedral mean the little streets are always busy. But it's lovely to ride through, and you'll be in a good mood as we continue up the coast, through Abereiddy and Trefin, past the ferries sailing from Fishguard across the Irish Sea to Rosslare.

It can get windy in these parts. It will do, when there's nothing between here and the east coast of Ireland except waves and big tides and fishing boats. But even when the sea breezes are buffeting you from the side, or it's overcast and cloudy, or if there's a drizzle coming in over the headlands, there is still something special about the landscape we're riding through. It's not quite a spiritual thing – maybe that's a bit wacky for a man who lives by power numbers and weight and average gradients – but it's a beautiful place, and we have time to appreciate it all.

We're staying in small lanes, much loved by farmers on quad bikes and tractors, so be careful at whatever time of year. If it's the end of summer and those farmers have been out trimming hedges or the weather's turned and there's mud and animal muck on the road, watch out for the thorns and the slippery stuff.

All of it adds to the adventure, but make sure you've checked your tyres for wear or nicks before you set off. Carry a couple of spare inner tubes. No-one deliberately gets a puncture, but there's a good chance you'll have at least one on this day. Take your time, treat it as part of the journey. A stop to change a tyre is also a chance to have a drink and snack from your back pocket, to get your heart-rate down or open a new line of conversation with your riding partner.

Onwards we go. From Cardigan the road is a good one, really up and down, but nice and smooth under your wheels. As we climb out of the town you can see the yellow curves of the beaches down below and then, out in front of you, all the little villages we're going to pass through before we finish in Aberaeron.

You could stay on the A487 all the way, but that would be boring and predictable, and today isn't about either. Instead we'll drop down to the coast at Aberporth, a straight steep descent, and then make a sharp right to the beach.

In need of sustenance? There's an ice-cream place here if you need something cooling, a fish and chip shop too if you're going to take your metabolism in your hands and risk a stomach full of heavy carbs before the long climb back out again. And it is a really long climb, too, all the way to the main road at Tan-y-groes. If it's taken more out of you than you ideally would have liked, panic not – there's a Londis a little further down the main road.

The tarmac ahead is a little lumpy here, so we'll take the left turn when we see the sign for Llangrannog, on to a long rolling descent with big views of the sea, two hairpins coming our way as the drop steepens. You'll go past the free park-and-ride car park and then left at St Carannog Church, past an old house on the edge of the cliff and the new statue of a 19th century woman called Cranogwen. Who was she? A poet, a preacher, a campaigner and the first woman to win a bardic prize at the National Eisteddfod. I'll admit I didn't know this in advance, but I do now and this is another reason to love riding in a new place. You explore the landscape and you explore all that shaped it too.

On a good clear day you can see right across to the grey and green mountains of Snowdonia from here. The day I rode it, I met Sa and Macs down by the beach, which is the ideal spot to rendezvous with your family or friends. It's a dead end, which makes this road the west Wales version of the famous Sa Calobra climb in Mallorca that I wrote about in *Mountains According to G*. What Sa Calobra doesn't have is an awesome wood-fired pizza place at the bottom, where you can take your food out onto the beach and refuel with the waves and wind out in front of you. It's called Tafell a Tân. You can't miss it.

That's the good news. The bad news is that the tricky narrow descent you've just freewheeled down is the same one you're going back up. It's horrible, whether you've got a bellyful of pizza or not. You're staying left at the church this time, along the B4321 through Pontgarreg, and it can take a good half-hour to winch your way back to the junction with the A487 again. We don't stay up there for long, though, diving left to drop down to Cwmtydu beach, the descent rolling rather than a plummet, and keeping the little twisting river on your left-hand side all the way. It's great down there with a quiet little sand-and-pebbles beach that not many know about. There's a tiny castle, Castell Bach, although it's more of tower really. Josh tells me this was the spot, probably in Cranogwen's time, where the beer and whisky and wine was smuggled in by locals and stashed in the castle to keep it from official view.

I'll be honest: the climb out again is probably the worst climb you'll do all day. There are S-bends, sections at 20%, a sense that it's at least double the 4km your Garmin might tell you. No wonder they left the beer down there – getting it home would be a nightmare. But appreciate these ancient narrow lanes for all they have to offer, for suffering up climbs you don't know is a blessing. It's all new: the road, the scenery, the random animals. Not knowing the top is still 1.5km away is better than knowing, right?

Maybe in peak school holiday time you'll be stopping for the occasional car, but at other times you'll have these roads to yourself. Sometimes you might feel lost, but the sea never moves position and the main road borders you on the other side. If you make a wrong turn simply turn around again. It's another road you might otherwise not have ridden, another twist in an adventure you've never had before.

For all those reasons, stay in the lanes from here rather than returning to the main road and the village of Synod Inn. We're aiming for New Quay, which will feel like quite the metropolis compared to Llangrannog. Go past all the campsites on the hills on the left and drop down by the car park, negotiating the hairpin at the bottom. Feel free to take in the vibes here. There's the Bluebell Deli and Bistro right on the beach, which Josh says is a winner, and there's a good cooked breakfast at Mariners, just round the corner, if you're reversing this route and going north to south instead. It's a great beach, too: white sand, two long sea walls to walk out along and boat trips for those who want to see it all from outside in.

The road back out is long but not too steep. It flattens off as we ride past the Quay West campsites on the left, and we'll follow the coast line until the road bends around through some woods and up to Llanarth. Past the Llanina Arms pub there's a lovely quick downhill section of about 500m. Go on past the Moody Cow farm shop (great burgers and a good soft play area for kids), and then it's downhill again all the way along the main road into Aberaeron.

You might get a block headwind on the long, fast descent, but don't let it get to you. Look ahead to see the other towns out along the coast – Aberarth, Aberystwyth.

See if you can spot a pod of bottlenose dolphins out in the bay. Give a wave to Ffos-y-ffin, where Josh grew up, and a nod to Tarling's Hill, the one Strava segment no-one else is allowed to get round here.

You want an ice-cream? Go to the Hive, where they make it using local honey rather than sugar. Enjoy a pint at the Harbourmaster pub and tuck in to fish and chips from the takeaway place with the blue awning. All great options, run by friendly, happy people.

On one ride round here I was out in the lanes, a little lost, happy enough but getting peckish and in need of a drink. I stopped at a local shop and the woman behind the counter recognised me. 'Geraint? I'm friends with so-and-so who knows your uncle. Congrats on your racing!' Now this was just after the Tour in 2021, arguably the least enjoyable Grand Tour – possibly even the least enjoyable race – of my entire career, but she wasn't to know that. I thanked her. As I left she added, 'Ah, Geraint, after what you've done, whatever you do now is fantastic. We all love you here.' It's strange, or maybe it isn't, but it felt like a massive boost to hear that from a random woman in a random shop in the middle of nowhere in west Wales. Great riding, even better people.

Oh – and one more thing, from the older generation to the young guns. Take a jacket with you on this ride. The weather changes fast out here. And take a lot of food. The climbs come at you quick and they won't let go. A lot changes in the world of cycling, but a lot stays the same, too.

# Riding with the Roches

**S**ometimes, when you're riding roads far from home, you fall into conversation with a team-mate and talk about other roads you have ridden. The ones you learned on, the ones you fell in love with, the ones that turned you over and the ones you never want to see again. The secret routes known only to you and those you trust.

So it was one day a few years ago riding out of Monaco with Nico Roche. Nico was with Sky for two fine years, in a career in which he did most things you could ever want to do on a bike: starting 24 Grand Tours, finishing 22 of them; twice Irish national champion; twice a stage winner at the Vuelta; an essential part of serious teams like BMC, Sunweb, Ag2R, Saxo-Tinkoff and Credit Agricole.

Nico's a great man to have alongside you on a bike. Good chat on him, well-travelled, likes his football, likes his rugby. Speaks French as well, as you'd expect from a kid with a French mother who spent big chunks of his childhood in her native land. He's also cycling royalty, Nico. His father Stephen was truly one of the greats, the only man – alongside Eddy Merckx – to win the Tour de France, Giro d'Italia and Worlds road race in the same year.

So it'll make sense why we're riding with the Roches today, out of Dublin and into the hills beyond. It's a classic route for any self-respecting rider in those parts. We'll start it at a place all the locals know: Marlay Park, right on the southern fringes of the city. It's backroads beside, and then under and past the motorway, following the R113 and cutting across Rockbrook before taking a left onto the R115 and then right on the R113 to Wood-stown village.

It's all good from here, the city falling away behind us and County Wicklow opening up in the distance. Along the R113 to Old Mill, then the R114 and out past Kiltipper Park and through Ballinascorney until we hit the N81, right opposite the Blue Gardenia pub.

The turns come quickly out here, but they're all good and the signposts can be relied upon. We're on the N81 only for a brief pedal, then we take the first left on to the R759 to take us through Kilbride, over a much smaller iteration of the Liffey than you'll see back in Dublin, and on to Woodend. You'll know you're in the right place as the road snakes its way south because you'll see all the water on your right, and so Lake Drive will carry us all the way through Lacken to the junction with the R758 and a left turn.

Turn left again at the next T-junction, on to the R756. Now the really good stuff is coming your way. This is the beginning of the climb called Wicklow Gap, and it's a beauty – the bottom part through the forests, and then opening up as you continue to ascend before it drops down again into Laragh.

The Irish roads feel familiar after growing up in Wales: generally small, twisty and heavy as anything. They make the roads of Mallorca or Italy feel like riding a wooden velodrome. However, my only prior experience of riding on roads like this came during the Junior Tour of Ireland. It was a massive race back in the day. I had to get special permission in 2002 to ride it as a 16-year-old, a year younger than you're meant to. God, how I suffered, but it was a quality field, with riders from the continent travelling over to race, and I loved it.

Hard gritty roads to go with the hard gritty racing. It rained most of the time and we were always covered in various types of muck. To my surprise – and to the surprise of the peloton I guess – I won the final stage with a late attack over a small climb in Waterford. Solo for 3km, racing like I had a pack of dogs at my rear wheel, all for a nice Waterford Crystal trophy that's still displayed proudly at my mum and dad's house. Some Irish guy with a famous dad won the race that year, while riding for the big French amateur team VC la Pomme. His name? Nicolas Roche. I remember thinking how big and strong he was. Every day, racing at the front, competing for the win. I couldn't work out how it could be possible. I was full gas just to finish among the also-rodes.

I entered the race again two years later, flying straight in from Los Angeles where I'd just won the scratch race at the Junior World Track Championships. Partly because of the jet lag, partly because we had the Junior World Road Race a few weeks later, I was told to take it easy on the first few days and then maybe race the last couple. Ian Stannard won, riding for Great Britain; sure enough, I followed my instructions and won the fifth stage of the six. My main memory was sitting on in the final, not wanting to help some Dutch rider called Gesink gain time and pass Stannard on GC. Both would turn out to be quite handy as their careers developed.

There were a few other Irish riders in the break that day as well. Up a little drag a few kilometres from the finish, a van came past with its sliding door fully open. A furious Irishman leaned out, hurling abuse at me for not working. I laughed, took off a few kilometres later and won the stage. I have no idea how angry he was at the finish. I didn't stick around to find out.

There's the option of a coffee stop here, at Glendalough Green. Nico tells me the place is run by an old lady who is something of a character, but that all is well because they have a love-hate relationship and both are just fine with it. Maybe she's related to the man in the van.

We head onwards, refreshed or otherwise, turning left onto Old Military Road, aka the R115. It cuts through the valley to begin with and then gradually transitions into the Glenmacnass climb. Keep an eye out for the waterfalls on your left; when you're right at the top of them turn further to your left to see the views stretching to Lough Ouler, Conavalla and County Kildare way out beyond.

It's a great road, this, according to Nico. One of his favourites anywhere, all the way to the top and the junction with Sally Gap. He's described it to me as looking like the classic Irish postcard: narrow lanes, climbing steeply; beautiful scenery. As we turn right onto the R759, it continues in the same vein, too – over the P.S. I Love You bridge (it's an Irish film reference) and past Lough Tay on your right as you drop down at pace to the next crossroads.

Another lively little road follows. It's Stoney Pass, an

up-and-down affair past the mountain-bike trail park at Ballinastoe Woods and the café with big portions they have there too, another waterfall on your left when rain has been in the air for weeks and big views across the hills to your right with the Irish Sea in the distance.

Onwards along the L1036, all the way to Enniskerry via Crowe Lane, and then a sharp left at the bridge to take in a little climb, only a kilometre or so in length, that the locals like to call the Irish Poggio. Now it doesn't look much like the actual Poggio, out on the Italian coast by San Remo, but we all map our cycling fantasies onto our own worlds and landscapes, so I'm absolutely buying into it. Nico used to do efforts on this hill; his best ever was 54 seconds, bottom to top, so give it a crack and see how you compare.

There's also a good coffee option in Enniskerry: Poppies, just past the police station. You may need the caffeine, for you have two options now. If you've done enough for the day, take the R117 to Kilternan and Stepaside Village and you'll be all the way back to Marlay Park in half an hour or so of good pedalling, almost all of it flat. Or, if you fancy another spicy little challenge, go back up the L1011 to Glencree for a beautiful short climb, stopping at the village's Centre for Peace and Reconciliation to learn a little more about the history and the culture you're riding through. From here it's right on the R115, taking you to the Killakee View Point for a spectacular view north and east across to Dublin. Right again onto the R116, and Marlay Park will come back to you – an extra hour in your legs, a bigger smile yet on your chops.

If you're fit – and fast – you've just clocked about four hours in total. How did it feel? Nico sold it to me well. We get all the traffic we need in Monaco and Nice and Cardiff. I can handle the idea of a few tourist buses. We're used to those from Tenerife. Rain? I'm from south Wales. I know all about cutting through the lanes and staying low when the heavy black clouds blow in.

It's the wild side of it I love. Nico's not naturally a poetic man, but when he talks about the sights and sounds out there in the Wicklow mountains, he's a rider transformed. The full force of nature out there atop Sally Gap, the four or five ways you can find to ride the same mountains from different directions and with varying pitch. It's a classic ride, waiting for us all to dive in and enjoy.

# Swifty and Cav's Mountain Man

There are places in this book I've known all my cycling life and places I first heard about from others. The Isle of Man, where my old friend and team-mate Mark Cavendish grew up and learned how to race his bike, and my friend and frequent team-mate Ben Swift went to live for a long chunk of his pro career, is one of the latter. What I love about it is that it has roads with big reputations and strange names, and new challenges for the rider who loves to be pushed.

It's not a big place, the Isle of Man, but the training possibilities are awesome. Just make sure you bring a good rain jacket. It might be slightly warmer than the mainland, but it's almost always wetter. It's often windy, too, and there can be times when proper weather blows in and it's horrific. Equally, when it's fifteen degrees and the sun is shining, it's one of the best places to ride your bike in the world.

So this is a loop to show us all that Swifty's adopted home and Cav's original manor can offer. It's a ride that clocks up 165km, but can be sliced and diced into most lengths. It has more than 3,100m of climbing in its original iteration, but is a cloth that can be cut to suit you.

On this ride, we climb Snaefell repeatedly, from multiple sides, with Snaefell dictating the strain our bodies are under. In its entirety it's a tough ride, one that could even strike fear into the locals, yet the views are awesome. The climbs are long and quiet, the isolation intense at times, but at least you're never too far from civilisation and a good coffee.

We begin in Onchan, just north of the capital, Douglas. Before we do, one aspect we are yet to discuss in this book is riding companions. Ideally they're slightly weaker than you, so you're boosted by being the stronger. However, if you're having an off-day, the feeling of your weaker partner handing your backside to you on a plate will always feel a hundred times worse.

The main attribute required? Decent chat. Even if they don't shut up, like Cam Wurf, you can zone out. Just don't chat on a climb when your partner is breathing out their arse. You also want someone with a bit of cycling etiquette, which means no half-wheeling for the majority of the time. Here on the Isle of Man you'll struggle to find someone without any chat. Maybe it's because it's a small island, but I'd say 95% of the cyclists I've met there have been confident, loud and brash. It's certainly entertaining. Topping it all off is the local accent: 60% Scouse, the other 40% something strange that happens nowhere else.

On the half-wheeling point, Cav is your main man. He's always been the same, starting each ride above threshold on every climb and sprinting over the top, with you thinking this might turn out to be a long day, especially if you're on a low-carb diet, as I have been for most of the past decade or so.

Anyway. Start off after breakfast, somewhere between 8.30 a.m. and 9.30 a.m., partly so you'll be riding the other way to the traffic coming into town and partly because this is a big day out if you're doing it all. It was just over six hours last time Swifty rode it, and Swifty can move. Swifty also doesn't often stop for coffee breaks. So head out on Hillberry Road and the rather appropriate Mountain Road, the A18, up to the Creg-Ny-Baa pub and then left as the road bends around. Go all the way up and then, just before Victory Café, take a left onto the A14, the summit of Snaefell high to our right.

Don't be freaked out if these roads seem quite main. It's the Isle of Man. The big roads are small roads. The small roads are tiny. Even the tractors on the smallest ones are infrequent and generous to passing cyclists. Yes, it's built up as you leave Douglas or Onchan, but it doesn't stay built up for long.

If you've ever watched the TT motorbike races on the island you'll recognise the Creg-Ny Baa, and there'll be a familiar feel to so many other twists and turns. As you swing to the left before the pub, you should be able to see Lancashire across the Irish Sea to the east.

As we keep climbing, first slowly on the steep sections at the bottom and then with a little more pace as the gradient drops over the top of the road towards the town of Ramsey in the north-east, you may even be able to see what the locals refer to as the six kingdoms – England, Scotland, Wales, Ireland, the Isle of Man and either the kingdom of the sea or the heavens above, depending on which version of the myth you prefer. You're right in the middle of it all here: 85 miles from Liverpool, 97 from Dublin, 31 to the Mull of Galloway in Scotland.

Past Sulby Reservoir on our left, past the forest of Tholt y Will Glen on our right and a plantation a little further on. There are strange wood carvings by the side of the road, reflecting the quirkiness of the island itself, and there are sheep grazing in the fields and on the verges, who will look up as they hear you coming and sometimes attempt to step into the road to get a closer look.

Up to Sulby itself and then right onto the A3 into Ramsey, where the TT bikes put the hammer down along the fast, smooth road surface. Cav will also push on down here, determined to show you how quick he can go, because these are his roads and also because he fancies himself as a motorbike rider. You can stop in Ramsey for coffee if you need it, which Swifty advises you might. There used to be a place called Conrod's on Parliament Street, but I've heard rumours it's closed now, so you may have to try Gophers or the Court Café.

The climb back out of Ramsey on the A18 is punchy at the start. You'll see Snaefell in front of you, although by the time you get closer you'll have done the hard yards – 9% in places, 7% a lot of the time. However, it's the third climb of the day that's the hardest, once we've followed the A18 almost back to Onchan but then cut across right along Scollag Road and then Ballaoates Road until we meet E Baldwin Road. It really kicks up when we turn west to pick up Ballamodha Road and then W Baldwin Road towards Injebreck. By now Cav's pace will be starting to falter, the energy bars and banana starting to kick in for me. Now you're riding next to him, no longer being half-wheeled. He doesn't like that so much. Even though you're not actually in front, merely level.

These are proper back lanes here, cut out through the trees, super-narrow and going up in a way that makes you think they'll never end. There are cattle grids at the bottom, trees bent sideways by the wind as you climb up to the exposed slopes. The wind round here can be so strong that the branches are almost formed in the teardrop shape of an aero helmet, the irony being that you're going so slowly at this point that there's no point in anything aero at all.

Be careful on the descents. The road surface is superb, but it's properly steep, and because you're dropping at pace the sheep that might wander into the road have far less time to react and scarper. When you hit the first proper junction it's left to Little London, then Kirk Michael on the east coast and a return to the familiar challenges of the TT course. When you head right at Ballaugh keep an eye out for the humpback bridge that the motorbikes hit at speed and get serious air, and then climb up Druidale. It's been re-tarmacked and is beautifully smooth, but that's the best we can say about it. It goes up arrow-straight, steeper than seems possible – 16% in places, a wonder of landscape and engineering melded together to push our legs to their limits.

From the end of the really steep bit to the very top of the climb is Swifty's favourite bit of road on the entire route. It's a road that's more of a track, past ancient abandoned stone cottages, a freezing stream burbling alongside you, just mountains and grass and sky all around you. It's like pedalling back through time, all the way to the strange house with a windmill at the very top, where there are always old cars on the drive being cannibalised and rebuilt.

Okay. Mind in the sort of state you want on an all-day epic, head back towards Brandywell Road, pick up the A18 again in the opposite direction to before and descend back down into Ramsey, views towards the Scottish coast across the ocean in front of you. We have two climbs to finish us (and Cav) off: we're doing several of the same roads more than once by this point, yet always a different way and with that a totally different feel. It's a relatively small geographical area we're covering, but it never feels like multiple loops, more like an A to B, and they're always the most fun.

The first is back up the A14, turning left off the A3 at Sulby, along to Tholt y Will Glen. You can see this one kick up in front of you, and as you reach the top and see our old friend Snaefell to your left again, Cav will now be half a wheel, maybe half a bike length behind as you really put the squeeze on him. He'll hate it. 'Lad, what are you doing?'

You should also be able to spot the electric railway that slowly winches non-riding tourists to the summit. It's always cool to see. Descend back to the junction with the A18 at Victory Café, turn right and then right again onto Beinn-y-Phott Road (don't say I didn't warn you about the strange names) and Brandywell to a quick loop around Spooyt Vane.

The way back past Little London on Brandywell heading east is pretty much our last big effort. Steep at the bottom, but only a short effort, views of England ahead of you this time as we retrace our tyre tracks to Onchan, maybe lobbing in a last cheeky diversion via Laxey for a final hurrah.

The last few miles are along very pleasant little lanes. You will probably be in pieces at this point. Cav will almost certainly have bonked by now and be completely wasted. That'll teach him. He won't do that again, at least not until 9 a.m. tomorrow when the whole process will start again, but you don't get as good as Swifty and Cav without putting the miles in. What you've knocked off today is as impressive as any mountain stage of the Tour de France, so enjoy tonight. Eat well. Allow yourself a pint or two or a glass of whisky. No-one on the entire Isle of Man will try to argue that you haven't earned it.

# Epilogue

**H**ere's the thing about loving riding your bike. There is always a new route to discover, an unknown road to pedal down, a fresh adventure ahead. And while I've been thinking about all the rides in this book, taking them on again in my mind or thinking about the next time I might point my handlebars down the road, zip up my jersey and clip in, I've been thinking about other rides, too.

Those rides are ones I've done or ones team-mates or friends have told me about. Mythical rides that get talked about whenever riders get together to talk – the ones that have you ordering an extra coffee, plotting it out on your Garmin, feeling that tickle in your guts that says you're part excited and part intimidated but absolutely in, all the way. So let's talk about some of those.

I came very close to telling you about the good times I had in my younger days on the Newport flats, cutting across east out of Cardiff into a land of low hedges and high winds, the River Severn just ahead, maybe a detour these days to St Tewdrics in Chepstow, the old manor house Sa and I took over and turned into a wedding venue. I thought about Box Hill in Surrey, and all the lanes that lead you there from south-west London and carry you on further into the Surrey Hills, and then the North Downs if you want them to. I rode them as we prepared for our tilt at team pursuit gold at the London Olympics of 2012 and, if you live in that part of London, odds are you've ridden them most weekends.

I thought about the Peak District. How us young Team GB track contenders used to pedal out of south Manchester and up the various wiggles and waggles into those green hills – the climbs that meet you everywhere, the tight descents, the hidden cafés and the rain, because for quite a lot of the winter you can't not think about the splatter on your clothing from the puddles and the muck on the smaller roads. I thought about Scotland and the adventures I had around Glasgow in winning the Commonwealth Games road race in 2014, the route they used for the Worlds road race and the time-trial in August 2023.

I could tell you about Andorra, now I've done a long training camp there, and by the end I got to understand its charms. I could tell you about the gravel ride Cam Wurf took me on in Los Angeles, showing me an entirely new side to the coastal mountains I thought I knew so well, or the charms of Portugal in early spring, or of Belgium's bergs and farm tracks when you're deep in Classics preparation.

If you knew what Tom Pidcock has told me about the secret routes through the Yorkshire Dales just north of where he grew up, you'd be over there in a flash. I'd happily open up a map and show you my Italy loop from Monaco, and where we've explored in Austria and Switzerland. I'd tell you about Isola, high in the French Alps, and all the challenges and thrills its altitude will throw at you.

And I'd enjoy hearing about your adventures too: the roads you know that I don't, the routes you've pieced together over different rides, the way to pedal them, the places to stop for coffee and cake. The moments and views as you ride through. Maybe you can let me know by showing them to me on social media or via the Geraint Thomas Cycling Club.

Because we're all in this together, especially at the end of a long day in the saddle. We ride for the same reasons and we experience the same pleasures. No matter how much you pay for it a bike is only a pair of wheels and some tubing, some rubber and some plastic. But oh, the places it can take you!

# Acknowledgements

I'd like to thank all the brilliant team at Quercus for their hard work, creativity and dedication, including Richard Milner, Dave Murphy, Chloë Johnson-Hill, Lipfon Tang, Keith Bambury and Jon Butler. It's always great forming a book breakaway with you.

Thank you to Lisa Hughes for her outstanding copy editing, to Bruce Doscher for all the cool artwork, and to David Luxton and Jay de Andrade for all their hard work behind the scenes.

Thanks and love to my family, especially Sa and Macs for putting up with my "extra-curricular" activity, and for all their support – especially when it comes to signing the pages, Macs! I couldn't do it without you.

And thank you to my co-writer and GTCC co-host Tom Fordyce. You're slower on a bike than me, and I can't type as fast as you. I think the partnership works well for both of us.